Caught in the
Middle East

Caught in the Middle East

Japan's Diplomacy in Transition

Michael M. Yoshitsu
University of Virginia

LexingtonBooks
D.C. Heath and Company
Lexington, Massachusetts
Toronto

Library of Congress Cataloging in Publication Data
Yoshitsu, Michael M.

  Caught in the Middle East.

  Includes index.
    1. Near East—Foreign relations—Japan.
  2. Japan—Foreign relations—Near East. I. Title.
  DS63.2.J3Y67 1984   327.56052   83–26805
  ISBN 0–669–08012–8 (alk. paper)

Published simultaneously in Canada

Printed in the United States of America

International Standard Book Number: 0–669–08012–8

Library of Congress Catalog Card Number: 83–26805

For Professor James William Morley

Contents

Preface

The Middle East has altered the direction of Japan's diplomacy. In Tokyo, dependence on Persian Gulf oil has locked key officials into a network of regional concerns that have transformed Japan's U.S.-centered foreign policy. The Japanese government departed sharply from such issues as auto exports and defense spending as Middle East threats to petroleum supplies posed a complex weave of problems whose solutions could not be forged with Washington alone. The Iran–Iraq War, Soviet aggression and Palestinian autonomy, the Japanese felt, required a broader range of responses that must be formulated with their European allies and the Gulf States.

This study analyzes Tokyo's search for a new pattern of diplomacy to quell the crises ignited by this new regional force. For the most part, it concentrates on Japan's ties to the Middle East after the Shah's exit from Teheran in early 1979. Events shaping Tokyo–Persian Gulf relations before then will be presented to provide a historic understanding of the contemporary situation.

The justification for this four-year analysis flows from the rapid redirection of strategic, economic and political currents in the Gulf area. For leaders in Japan, the shift of Soviet military activity from Angola to Afghanistan, the spread of Moslem revolution throughout Iran, and fluctuations in the volume of oil supply from individual producers turned policymaking into a forty-eight-month nightmare. The result was a gradual diplomatic swing away from the United States toward Western Europe, Saudi Arabia, Iran, Egypt, and the PLO.

Chapter 1 sets off the study with an analysis of the 1973 oil embargo and Japan's new Middle East diplomacy. The sudden loss of energy supplies, it contends, induced a structural change in Tokyo's foreign relations. No longer able to count on the major oil companies for automatic imports, the Japanese had to deal directly with the producer states and the regional problems confronting them.

The following four chapters target separate incidents and individual actors that triggered particular diplomatic responses. Chapter 2 first traces Tokyo's emerging relations with the Palestine Liberation Organization and its movement, together with Western Europe and Egypt, as they sought to discover a comprehensive peace plan that would include the PLO and establish a Palestinian state.

Chapter 3 reviews the impact of the U.S. hostage crisis on Tokyo's foreign relations, centering on Japan's efforts to safeguard Iran from superpower intervention and internal collapse through ties to Western Europe and Teheran. Chapter 4 analyzes Japan's response to Soviet aggression in Afghanistan. The Olympic boycott, trade cutoffs and other measures, it shows, represented a diplomatic attempt to deter the Soviets until a Western tripwire could be set.

Finally, chapter 5 assesses Tokyo's reaction to the Iran–Iraq War, pointing to renewed anxiety in Japan over Teheran's fall as the impetus for decisions to work with Japanese business and Iran in completing a multibillion dollar petrochemical project near Abadan. The study then concludes with a set of general observations that place Japan's new diplomacy in a broad theoretical context.

On one level, the book was written to explain the emergence of Japan–Persian Gulf ties. But on another, it was done to present a more fundamental, ongoing shift in Tokyo's foreign relations with the United States. Throughout the post-World War II period, the Japanese had defined national survival in a bilateral context. The relationship with Washington, they felt, had provided a shield under which they could develop their resources and eventually emerge as an equal member of the Western alliance. In Tokyo, military security, economic stability, and international acceptance were thus policy lines linking Japan directly to the United States. But in the 1970s, this changed.

During the post-OPEC period, the management of strategic, economic, and political issues vitally affecting Japan clearly fell outside the Washington relationship. Not only did responses to the Arab/Israeli conflict, Soviet presence in Afghanistan, and turmoil in Iran require a broader array of participants, but they also underscored diverging interests that placed Tokyo and Western Europe at odds with the United States. The result in Japan was a precarious balancing act, with senior officials holding onto traditional ties to America and yet forced to act alone in dealing with threats to their nation and continuing relations with the United States.

In presenting this period of uncertain transition in Japan's diplomacy, this book relies heavily on information gleaned from personal interviews with many primary policymakers. A partial list of officials includes:

Former Prime Minister Takeo Miki

Former Foreign Ministers Saburo Okita, Toshio Kimura and Iichiro Hatoyama

Former Vice Ministers of Foreign Affairs Fumihiko Togo, Shinsaku Hogen and Masuo Takashima

Former Deputy Director of the Foreign Ministry Middle East–Southwest Asia Bureau Koichi Tsutsumi

Former Vice Minister for International Affairs Naohiro Amaya, the Ministry of International Trade and Industry

Former Vice Minister for International Affairs Takehiro Sagami, the Ministry of Finance.

Because of the sensitivity of this topic, other important sources have preferred to remain anonymous. The author must therefore ask for the reader's understanding of the restrictions under which *Caught in the Middle East* was written.

Acknowledgments

The author is deeply grateful to many institutions and individuals for their kind assistance. Financial support from the Fulbright Commission, American Philosophical Society, Ellen Bayard Weedon Foundation and University of Virginia provided several opportunities to conduct research in Tokyo. Comments by Professors R.K. Ramazani of the University of Virginia and Professors James William Morley and Gerald L. Curtis of Columbia University helped shape the manuscript.

Thanks are also due Professor Takeshi Igarashi of Tokyo University and Mr. Noritada Otaki of the National Diet Library for facilitating research arrangements in Japan, and *The New York Times* and University of California Press for permission to incorporate earlier articles in this study.

The author bears sole responsibility for all fact and interpretation contained herein.

1

The Oil Embargo and Japan's New Middle East Diplomacy

We did not have a grand, well-designed diplomacy toward the Middle East at that time . . . [because] before 1973 we could always buy the oil if we only had the money. —Fumihiko Togo, former Japanese ambassador to the United States[1]

The 1973 Arab oil embargo pinpointed the paradox in Japan's foreign relations with the Middle East. Tokyo had an identifiable policy toward the Persian Gulf area, but it lacked a diplomacy to give that policy an identity in the area. Prior to November 1973, the Japanese government had embraced two interrelated positions on the Arab-Israeli conflict. With the United States and Western European countries, Tokyo had backed United Nations Resolution 242 (November 22, 1967), which called on Israel to withdraw from areas captured during the October 1967 war. Again voting with the majority, Tokyo had supported Resolution 2628 (November 4, 1970), which equated respect for Palestinian rights with a just and lasting settlement of the situation in the Middle East.

Senior officials had constructed these twin pillars of Persian Gulf policy, believing them to be the minimal requirements for peace in the region. Nevertheless, they had refrained from fusing the two elements into one comprehensive statement. "Japan's positions," one official acknowledged, "were scattered all about." Moreover, Tokyo planners had informed only one Persian Gulf leader, King Faisal of Saudi Arabia, of their views on Israeli withdrawal and the Palestinian issue. As a result, "the Arab countries were largely unaware of [Japan's] recognition of the legitimate right of Palestinian self-determination."[2]

The emergence of policy in a vacuum was neither odd nor inconsistent with Japanese interests in the Middle East. Although the Arab-Israeli conflict presented one set of concerns, it had remained divorced from the matter of securing stable energy supplies in the region. Until late 1973, Tokyo had regarded Cal-Tex, Mobil, Exxon, and other major oil companies as the conduit for Middle Eastern crude oil, which amounted to 81 percent of total petroleum imports. Thus, for the Japanese, the governments of the Gulf area were irrelevant parts of their energy equation. According to one official:

We were heavily dependent on Middle Eastern oil. But who supplied

1

the oil to us? Certainly not the Middle Eastern countries . . . but the so-called major oil companies. [Therefore] the only parties we had to deal with were the producing countries that were not in the Middle East.[3]

From October 1973, however, that would no longer be possible. On October 7, full-scale war erupted, with Israel fighting Egypt along the Suez Canal and Syria in the Golan Heights. Eight days later, Saudi Arabia responded by undertaking an economic counteroffensive against Tel Aviv. Speaking before Western executives, the Saudi oil minister, Sheikh A.Z. Yamani, reportedly said that his country would roll back crude oil production by 10 percent at once and by 5 percent each month thereafter should the United States resupply Israeli forces. Then, on October 21, the other members of the Organization of Arab Petroleum Exporting Countries (OAPEC) joined the Saudis in imposing a total ban on oil exports to the United States and reducing their production by 5 percent a month. Three days later, Riyadh officially informed Japanese executives from ARAMCO and seven other firms of the restrictions that had been in effect since the eighteenth.[4]

What made all of this especially painful for Japan was the uneven nature of the production cutbacks and distribution system, which magnified the impact of the oil embargo. The relationship between Gulf Oil and Kuwait was a prime example. Gulf, the fourth largest major oil company in Japan, had depended on Kuwait for 60 percent of its petroleum. To cope with dwindling supplies there and elsewhere, Gulf informed Tokyo customers on October 29 that it would immediately slash shipments to them by 35 percent—nearly 3 percent of Japan's total imports.[5] The other oil companies acted similarly, covering their major, minor, and overlapping losses with broad, across-the-board reductions to Japan. The combined effect, according to foreign ministry estimates, was a November and December shortfall approaching 40 percent. Within the foreign ministry, there seemed to be a feeling that the country could manage somehow for two or three months, given the fifty-two-day oil reserve on hand and the additional twenty-seven day supply in tankers en route to Japan.[6] Beyond that, however, the situation would become critical.

For the ministry, the cutbacks appeared to have another, equally dark, side. Although senior planners were chiefly concerned about import volume, they also began to worry about oil price. Fears of further reductions had ignited panic buying that involved private Japanese firms and the government of Libya. The contracts drawn up between those parties had stipulated quantity sold but had conspicuously omitted purchase price. Through its own sources, the foreign ministry had learned that the amounts paid were exorbitant and, at least in one instance, exceeded the going rate by several times. Senior officials concluded that these firms would use the strength of the Japanese economy to cover their costs and, in so doing, induce rampant inflation that would eventually impede economic growth.[7] Turning on the oil thus seemed to mean domestic control as well as international survival.

In the prime minister's office, Kakuei Tanaka reacted to the start of the embargo by telling advisors, "This is horrendous, this is horrendous."[8] Evidently not knowing what to do, he delegated decision-making responsibility to Foreign Minister Masayoshi Ohira and his principal subordinate—Vice-Minister Shinsaku Hogen and Deputy Minister Fumihiko Togo.

In late October, these officials first marked off the endpoints of their policy line on the oil crisis. At one extreme was the decision to maintain full diplomatic relations with Israel. Since the middle of the month, they had heard calls from business circles for an abrogation of ties to Tel Aviv. Only such strong action, the ministry leaders had been told, would mollify OAPEC members. Ohira, Hogen, and Togo strongly disagreed, dismissing those individuals as "people with oil on the brain."[9] In their view, Israel was an ally. Moreover, the requirement of consistent foreign relations meant that "Japan could not change its policy toward Israel overnight just because of the Arab situation."[10] Clearly, the Japanese-Israeli alliance would have to stay intact.

At the other extreme was the decision regarding the Arab world itself. Initially, the three men agreed that they could not overstep the perimeters of existing policy—namely, Tokyo's support for the two United Nations resolutions. As Hogen recalled, "abiding by 242 in particular was the best that we could do."[11] The three men apparently concluded that anything more would directly affect Tokyo's commitment to Tel Aviv.

Having defined these two policy limits, Ohira, Hogen, and Togo began to fill in their policy details. They first decided to win favor with OAPEC members by informing Gulf leaders of Japan's support for the Arab cause. On October 19, they had their first opportunity.

At that time, Arab ambassadors to Tokyo visited Ohira at the foreign ministry. As spokesman for the group, Saudi representative Dejani urged Japan "to positively support the Arab position on the Middle East conflict." The foreign minister responded by reminding the diplomats of Japan's vote on Resolution 242 and by pledging his government's continuing effort to implement the resolution at the United Nations.[12]

On October 26, Dejani returned to the foreign ministry for a private session with Hogen. During that meeting, the vice-minister reiterated Tokyo's support for Resolution 242 and handed the Saudi ambassador

"A Statement of Japan's Position on the Fourth Middle East War."
This document stipulated (1) that Israeli forces must withdraw from all
areas occupied after the October 1967 war, (2) that any settlement of
the conflict must respect the legitimate right of Palestinian self-determination, and (3) that the Japanese government would reexamine policy toward Israel should that country ignore the three principles.[13]

Reflecting on the document, Hogen emphasized that "nothing had
really changed. . . . Of course, the newspapers [in November] said
that we had hastily reformulated our thinking on the Middle East. That,
however, was not the case . . . [for] we had no intention of changing
our policy."[14]

In a strict sense, the vice-minister was correct. The statement on
the fourth Middle East war had incorporated the United Nations resolutions that Japan had supported in 1967 and 1970. Moreover, the
final point on policy toward Israel had promised reexamination, not
punishment. From a broader perspective, however, much had changed.
For the first time, the government had drafted a complete list of views
on the Middle East and then had tried to transmit it to officials in the
Arab world. During the next several weeks, other parts of this new
diplomacy would come to light.

From mid-November, Tokyo officials dealt with a different regional
force, which could hamper their efforts in the Gulf area. In the foreign
ministry, there was growing concern that economic strain engendered
by the oil embargo had accentuated long-standing differences with the
United States over Middle East policy. Before October 1973, divergent
views on occupied Arab territories and Palestinian rights could be ignored as a general problem that did not directly impinge on Japan's
foreign relations. After October, however, the luxury of oversight quickly
vanished with Tokyo's attempt to reach out toward Persian Gulf leaders. For senior officials, the question was how to avoid a diplomatic
rift with Washington that might delimit their area of maneuverability
in the region.

Until mid-December, the prime minister and the foreign minister
tried to dampen two potential flash points in relations with their most
important ally. Both concerns, Israel and energy policy, were raised
during Secretary of State Henry Kissinger's meetings with Ohira on
November 14 and with Tanaka on November 15. The statements by
the two Japanese, as well as later official reaction, revealed selective
use of bluntness and ambiguity in handling these issues.

In talks with the Secretary, Tanaka and Ohira couched their explanation of views on the Arab-Israeli conflict in terms of domestic
hardship. While apprising Kissinger of their statement on the fourth
Middle East war, the two leaders emphasized that Japan's great de-

pendence on Persian Gulf petroleum and the major oil companies had combined with the embargo to produce an economic crisis. Moreover, Tanaka praised Washington for its efforts on the October 22 ceasefire and promised to support the United States at the United Nations. He added, however, that only recognition of Arab demands regarding the implementation of Resolution 242 would permanently end the conflict that had led to petroleum losses.[15] By stressing resource vulnerability, the prime minister and the foreign minister evidently hoped to win reluctant acceptance or at least to minimize U.S. criticism of their diplomacy toward the Middle East.

The second concern, energy policy, related to the Secretary's proposal for a consortium of oil-consuming nations. The Japanese were clearly unenthusiastic, first judging that the appearance of an anti-OAPEC front might provoke a sharp Arab response. Apparently underscoring the hazard of this proposal was Sheikh Yamani's threat of November 19 to counter joint Japanese, U.S., and Western European actions with an immediate 80 percent cut in Saudi production.[16] Another reason for opposition emanated from the belief that the plan offered too little, too late. "It might help us weather short-term emergencies," Hogen explained, "but the proposal by itself would not solve the problem of long-term dependence. For that, we would have to look to other measures."[17] As his official response, Ohira therefore chose to avoid a yes or no that would antagonize either Washington or the Arab world. In a statement on December 14, the foreign minister simply said that "the Kissinger concept would have to be clarified."

Parallel to Japan's response to the United States was a new round of initiatives toward the Persian Gulf countries. Following the November 4 OAPEC decision to raise cutbacks to 25 percent, the Saudi government used a Japanese intermediary, Sohei Mizuno (president of Arabian Oil-Japan), to convey a message to the prime minister. During a meeting with Tanaka on November 19, Mizuno stressed Riyadh's wish for a clear indication of policy change toward Israel. Tokyo's action, the businessman continued, would have to be taken before the November 24 start of the Arab foreign ministers' conference; otherwise, Riyadh would have no choice but to view Japan as an enemy. Mizuno then warned that refusal to respond positively might lead to further Saudi cutbacks, if not a total OAPEC ban against Japan.[18]

The message evidently prompted one decision and reinforced another. Amid great fanfare, Chief Cabinet Secretary Susumu Nikaido issued an official statement of government policy toward the Middle East. Apart from the title, the document of November 22 repeated verbatim Hogen's "Statement of Japan's Position on the Fourth Middle East War." Tokyo officials apparently hoped that international publicity given the release would suggest the policy break that Riyadh had wanted. Nevertheless, the foreign ministry continued to feel that "nothing had really changed."[19] In the view of Ohira, Hogen, and Togo, the statement was part of their effort to enhance Gulf State relations in a way that would preserve ties to Israel.

The second decision, though more involved, also aimed at the same objective. In early November, when the cutbacks began to be felt, Ohira and his subordinates first considered sending a special emissary from the government to the Middle East. That individual, they initially agreed, would try to end the embargo by persuading Arab leaders that Japan "was a friend, not a foe."[20] Within the foreign ministry, however, other officials expressed strong reservations. According to them, Middle Eastern countries might use the visit as a chance to vent their anger or impose unreasonable demands on Japan. This, they feared, would lead to a conflict pitting Tokyo more directly against the Arab world.

Though aware of this argument, the prime minister nevertheless decided to support his foreign minister. Tanaka believed that something needed to be done. By mid-November, he selected a personal envoy whose political views were largely incompatible with his own. That, however, appeared to be the principal appeal of Vice-Premier Takeo Miki.

As one inside source observed:

> Japan was facing a grave economic crisis. And the selection of a special representative became an important issue, since that person would be entrusted with the task of ending the oil embargo against Japan. This was of course the major test of the Tanaka Cabinet [in late 1973] . . . . It seems that the prime minister therefore decided to go with the person who might have the greatest understanding of the Arab world. . . . Within the [ruling] Liberal-Democratic Party, Miki stood out as a leader of the progressive wing. And so Tanaka apparently felt that Miki would have the best chance of establishing a rapport with the Middle Eastern leaders. . . . We can certainly see this today [in 1981]. Whenever Arab officials come to Japan, they always want to meet one politician more than anybody else—[former] Prime Minister Miki.[21]

Following this decision, Ohira and Hogen met Miki to discuss the Middle East trip. Although they did not hand him a formal set of instructions, the two planners "suggested what [the vice premier] might say and whom he might see."[22] The foreign minister and the vice-minister first wanted Miki to inform Arab leaders of Japan's policies toward the Gulf area. In their judgment, the vice-premier should stress Tokyo's positions on Palestinian rights—particularly its vote on Resolution 242.

Besides words of support, Ohira empowered Miki with another, more tangible tool of persuasion. At his descretion, the vice-premier could extend development assistance to the countries he would visit. Since late October, senior officials had expected OAPEC members to condition normal oil flow on grants-in-aid from Japan. The Saudi ambassador did not broach the subject of technical help during his October 26 meeting with Hogen. Nevertheless, the vice-minister "would not have been surprised had he done so" for, in Tokyo's view, Japan and the Gulf States had what one another wanted. An energy-for-expertise trade-off therefore seemed to be natural. Then, in November, the natural became inevitable, when ambassadors from the Middle Eastern countries evidently gave the Japanese their shopping lists of economic demands.

Clearly, the foreign ministry felt that it could not afford to refuse. As one official recalled:

> Suddenly the oil shock came and we didn't know how to keep or maintain [our] friendship with the Middle Eastern countries. If they asked for economic assistance . . . we believed that we would have to do whatever was possible. And so we promised to help them.[23]

Despite this tilt toward aid, Ohira and his subordinates continued to worry about one part of Japan's response. As far as they were concerned, Tokyo was quite willing "to do whatever was possible," but it could not do whatever the Arab countries demanded. "The Japanese government," Hogen emphasized, "was unable to do everything. . . . Most of the projects would ultimately have to be undertaken by the private sector. And [we feared] that they did not understand the social, political and business conditions of our country . . . or would pretend not to."[24] The need to explain those conditions led to the appointment of Saburo Okita (president of the Japan Overseas Economic Development Fund), a noted economist, who would ostensibly assist the case-by-case review of all Arab requests.

Finally, foreign ministry officials considered which countries the vice-premier should visit. Obviously, Saudi Arabia and Egypt were most important, since the former had been the prime mover behind the embargo and the latter had been the major Arab participant in the war leading to the embargo. In addition, "special priority was also placed on Iran." In Japan, Shah Pahlavi had been widely regarded as a friend "who was firmly in control."[25] In mid-October, for example, he had assured Tokyo that his country would not join any oil freeze against Japan. The Iranian leader thus perfectly fit the broad description of a Japanese ally. As one official commented: "There is always the question whether the present government is the best government. [But] in international politics . . . that a government is basically friendly, basically dependable is all that counts.''[26]

The last four countries added to Miki's schedule occupied neither the leadership position of Saudi Arabia and Egypt nor the friendship status of Iran, yet they seemed to be important. Syria had been the other Arab combatant in the recent conflict, whereas Kuwait, Qatar, and the United Arab Emirates appeared to represent more moderate elements in OAPEC. Because of these contrasting considerations, the foreign ministry evidently thought the four countries to be worth the potential costs of an official visit.

On December 8, the vice-premier departed for the Middle East, accompanied by Togo, Okita, and several other advisors. The two bargaining chips in their possession were played effectively throughout the eighteen-day trip. The first, Japan's policies toward the Arab world, won strong approval from Gulf State leaders whom the vice-premier met. Generally, Togo recalled, "Miki [and the rest of us] went to inform them what Japan would and could do. . . . We were very concerned whether they would view Japan as a good guy or a bad guy. Because of our policies, they said that Japan was definitely not a bad guy.[27]

The favorable Arab response was especially evident during Miki's meetings with officials in Riyadh. On December 12, the vice-premier "explained [Japan's] policies at great length . . . [since] there were clearly aspects that they did and did not understand.''[28] The Saudi vice-president reacted by praising Japan for its position on the Palestinian issue and clarification of its past support for Resolution 242. Later in the day, King Faisal went a step further. After hearing Miki's statement on the suffering caused by the embargo, the Saudi leader promised to work toward helping his friends in Japan.[29]

Reaction in the other Arab capitals was equally positive. The United Arab Emirates president, for example, thanked Tokyo for its "first step toward a new Mideast policy," while the Syrian vice-president said Japan's stance had brought the two Asian countries closer together.[30]

Still, there appeared to be one point of difference. Throughout the Miki mission, Togo noted, "Arab leaders had some rather nasty things to say about Israel . . . but none of them demanded a diplomatic break [with Israel].''[31] On December 18, though, the Egyptian president came closest when he asked Miki to consider a cessation or suspension of economic relations with Tel Aviv.[32] Apparently wishing neither to punish Israel nor to argue with Egyptian President Anwar el-Sadat, the Japanese vice-premier gave a vague response. During a press conference held the next day, Miki said that any reexamination of policy toward Israel could occur only after his return to Japan and discussion of the matter with Prime Minister Tanaka.[33] Under the circumstances, Miki may have judged that the safest answer was no answer at all.

The second bargaining chip, development assistance, was used most where the stakes were highest. On December 14, Okita and other Japanese specialists started discussions with Saudi representatives on four separate refinery, petrochemical, mining, and steel projects that Riyadh wanted.[34] Although negotiations would have to continue into the future, they initially established the quid pro quo that Tokyo wanted.

In Cairo, the pattern continued. The Japanese group headed by Okita made the largest firm commitment of the trip, offering a $280 million government pledge to help expand and modernize the Suez Canal. Then, in Teheran, Vice-Premier Miki heard a general request from the shah for help in developing his country.[35]

On December 25, the Miki mission and the Japanese government received what they wanted most. The OAPEC members, meeting in Kuwait, recognized the Philippines, Belgium, and Japan as friendly countries. While deciding to continue the total ban against the United States and the Netherlands, they announced plans to cancel the 5 percent cutback set for January and to schedule a 10 percent increase instead.

In Tokyo's perspective, the mission had succeeded. Using past policy as a foundation, senior officals believed they had built a diplomacy that ended the embargo against Japan. As subsequent events would show, however, what was done in late 1973 was just a beginning. From 1974, and particularly after 1979, old problems and new developments merged to create pressure for a diplomacy strong enough to meet Arab demands yet flexible enough to protect a more complex set of Persian Gulf interests. What follows is an account of how the Japanese responded and remained caught in the Middle East.

Notes

1. Personal interview with Fumihiko Togo, former Japanese ambassador to the United States, July 21, 1981.

2. Personal interview with a high-ranking Japanese official (hereafter cited as Source A), August 1982.

3. Personal interview with Koichi Tsutsumi, former deputy director of the Middle East and Southwest Asia Bureau, Ministry of Foreign Affairs, July 17, 1981.

4. "Sauji Arabia, Nihon Hassha Tsukoku," *Asahi Shimbun,* October 25, 1973, p. 1.

5. Ibid.

6. "Bichikuryo wa nanajyu nichibun," *Asahi Shimbun,* October 17, 1973, p. 9.

7. Personal interview with a high-ranking Japanese official, June 1981.

8. Interview with Togo.

9. Interview with Togo.

10. Personal interview with Shinsaku Hogen, former Vice Minister, Ministry of Foreign Affairs, July 16, 1981.

11. Ibid.

12. "Arabu Taishidan Gaiso Ni Hyomei," *Asahi Shimbun* (evening edition), October 19, 1973, p. 1.

13. Interview with Source A. See also "Shinarabu E Seifu Kenkai," *Asahi Shimbun,* November 29, 1973, p. 1.

14. Interview with Hogen.

15. "Gaiso Kichokan To Kaidan" and "Kichokan Nihon Ni Seikan Yosei," *Asahi Shimbun,* November 15, 1973, p. 1, and November 16, 1973, p. 1.

16. "OPEC Arabu Kakuryo Genmei," *Asahi Shimbun,* November 20, 1973, p. 1.

17. Interview with Hogen.

18. "Arabu Seikishacho, Shusho Ni Hokoku," *Asahi Shumbun,* November 20, 1973, p. 1.

19. Interview with Hogen.

20. Interview with Hogen.

21. Interview with Source A.

22. Interview with Hogen.

23. Interview with Tsutsumi.

24. Interview with Hogen.

25. Interview with Hogen.

26. Personal interview with a high-ranking Japanese official, July 1981.

27. Interview with Togo.

28. Personal interview with Takeo Miki, former prime minister of Japan, July 29, 1981.

29. "Dai Ippo Toshite Hyoka" and "Faiseru Kokuo To Kaiden," *Asahi Shimbun,* December 12, 1973, p. 1, and December 13, 1973, p. 1.

30. "Arabu Shiji Meikaku" and "Shiriya Mo Yukoteki," *Asahi Shimbun,* December 11, 1973, p. 2, and December 24, 1973, p. 1.

31. Interview with Togo.

32. "Miki Sadato Kaidan," *Asahi Shumbun,* December 22, 1973, p. 2.

33. Ibid.

34. "Seiyu Shisetsu Nado Yon Jigyo," *Asahi Shimbun,* December 15, 1973, p. 1.

35. "Miki Tokushi Ni Keizairyoku," *Asahi Shumbun,* December 27, 1973, p. 7.

2

Middle East Peace
Through the PLO Prism

Peace in the Middle East is not something that can or cannot be achieved.
It must be achieved . . . [for] the region is more than an energy problem.
It is a political, strategic and economic problem.   —Takeo Miki,
former prime minister of Japan[1]

The Palestine Liberation Organization (PLO) was a lightning rod for
Japanese concerns about peace in the Middle East. In Tokyo's view,
the PLO stood at the center of the issue that posed the greatest threat
to long-term stability in the Persian Gulf region. Palestinian rights, the
Japanese judged, not only represented open conflict between Israel and
the Arab world but also symbolized a line separating the Gulf States
from the West. For leaders in Tokyo, failure to forge a lasting solution
would perpetuate two-party warfare and Allied weakness in an area
susceptible to revolutionary change, cross-border fighting, and Soviet
penetration.

From the mid-1970s, as their response to the absence of a comprehensive settlement, senior officials moved steadily toward the PLO.
On November 23, 1974, Tokyo leaders took their first tentative step
at the United Nations General Assembly (UNGA). During the twenty-
ninth session of the UNGA, delegates from the Gulf States and other
countries introduced two resolutions supporting self-determination for
the Palestinian people and proposing observer status for the PLO. The
position of the Japanese government reflected something new and
something old in its thinking.

Initially, Tokyo leaders favored both measures. Palestinian rights
had already been established as a principle of their foreign policy, and
observer status for the PLO seemed logical and desirable. The latter
measure, they felt, "was just an affirmation of the PLO's history and
status in the Arab world."[2] After all, the Arab Summit Conference
had decided on October 28, 1974, to designate the PLO "the sole and
legitimate" representative of all Palestinian people. Moreover, the Japanese clearly hoped that the PLO's presence at the world body would
facilitate informal dialogue with Israel and might open discussion among
the parties most concerned over the Arab-Israeli dispute.

Despite this predisposition toward a yes vote, the Japanese ambassador cast two abstentions. The reason for the first was the need to

retain a balance with Israel and the Arab world. Particularly disturbing to Foreign Minister Toshio Kimura, Vice-Minister Fumihiko Togo, and members of the Middle East Bureau was the omission in the self-determination resolution of a reference to Israel's right to exist. As one policy planner explained: "We always abstain if a resolution does not give sufficient regard to the position of Israel or is [otherwise] one-sided."

After this vote, Ambassador Shizuo Saito tried to lessen the sting of Japan's position to the Arab world. Citing Tokyo's long-standing support of Palestinian rights, he emphasized that abstention should not be construed as rejection. Indeed, Tokyo was in "full agreement with the principle and spirit" of the resolution. Unfortunately, though, it had failed to reaffirm UN Resolution 242, which stipulated the rights of Israel and other principles basic to a peaceful solution of the Middle East problem.[3]

In contrast, the problem with the second resolution related to what it contained. According to one source: "The Arab countries introduced the observer status measure in a way that would treat the PLO as a country instead of some [nongovernmental] organization like the IMF. A 'yes' would therefore mean diplomatic relations with the PLO and this would create other problems for us."[4] Under the circumstances, Japan had little choice but to abstain again.

Three months later, the Foreign Ministry would alter this course by veering toward a diplomacy of direct contact with the PLO. This movement into high-policy gear resulted from an unexpected turn of electoral events in Japan. On December 9, 1974, Takeo Miki became the eleventh prime minister of the postwar period. Evidently no one was more surprised than Takeo Miki.

From October 1974, the political fortunes of Prime Minister Kakuei Tanaka had plummeted following news reports that grimly detailed a pattern of corporate payoffs for chief executive decisions. When the so-called Lockheed scandal forced Tanaka to resign on November 26, the stage seemed to be set for a violent intraparty clash over succession between the two front-runners, Masayoshi Ohira and Takeo Fukuda. The fear of bloodletting that could weaken the ruling Liberal-Democratic Party (LDP) caused the LDP vice-president, Etsusaburo Shiina, to take the initiative in supporting the candidacy of Takeo Miki. To the apparent chagrin of Ohira and Fukuda, LDP members quickly coalesced around a Miki prime ministership, believing it to be the ceasefire that the party needed.

The chance election of Miki, the politically weakest and ideologically most liberal faction leader in the party, set into motion a strong Palestinian policy based on moral concern and practical need. Appearing before the Diet on February 5, 1975, the prime minister opened the door to bridge-building between Tokyo and the PLO. While noting the recent UN decision to grant the PLO observer status, Miki said the government would be "willing to entertain a request from that organization for an office in Tokyo." At the same time, he emphasized that his administration was "not in a position to recognize [the PLO] diplomatically as a nation."[5]

The reason for Miki's offer of an office was linked to an unusual mix of policy ingredients that included right versus wrong, the Palestinian people, and U.S. policy toward Communist China. As foreign minister in 1967, Miki had strongly supported UN Resolution 242. In his judgment, Japan could never condone the use of military force for territorial gain. To the new prime minister:

> The heart of 242 was the statement that prohibited the expansion of areas by military means and called upon Israel to withdraw its troops from Arab lands occupied [after the 1967 war]. Japanese support for 242 did not indicate a change of policy brought about by the problems in the Middle East. It was a basic part of our way of thinking . . . that the expansion of territories by force could never be permitted . . . and that when it occurred, the occupying power should of course be required to leave.[6]

The oil embargo in 1973 had only deepened this conviction on the need for Israeli withdrawal. The prime minister believed that producer states had imposed export sanctions in reaction to U.S. inaction on the Palestinian issue. The Middle Eastern countries, according to Miki's assessment, believed that Washington's support for Resolution 242 in 1967 had been negated by its subsequent refusal to work for Israeli compliance. In his estimate, the Arab world believed that "America alone had great influence on Israel. . . . And as far as they were concerned, it was not enough for the U.S. to vote for 242 but to refrain from implementing it. They therefore chose to use oil as a weapon and focus world attention on the plight of the Palestinian refugees, who are scattered all over the Middle East."[7]

What translated Miki's interest in Palestinian rights into an offer of a PLO office was the belief that "the organization represented the Palestinian people." The prime minister evidently believed that direct contact with the PLO would enable Japan to establish friendship with a larger group, whose fate would determine the fate of the Persian Gulf region itself. In addition, direct contact might serve another, more distant purpose. To Miki, only agreement among the United States, Israel, Egypt, Saudi Arabia, Jordan, Syria, and the PLO on a Palestinian homeland would bring permanent peace. Should this breakthrough occur, Japan "could contribute to the stability of the area set aside for the Palestinian people . . . with industrial and financial assistance."[8] Under this scenario, a PLO office could arguably become Tokyo's conduit for the aid packages that would boost any comprehensive settlement.

Another factor prompting Miki's decision had little to do with events in the Persian Gulf area. In the prime minister's office, the Foreign Ministry, and the Liberal-Democratic Party, there was widespread fear that the PLO might become "Japan's second China."

Until mid-1971, Japanese officials had heard U.S. presidents proclaiming adherence to a policy of nonrecognition toward the People's Republic of China. Despite strong public protest, Tokyo had decided to follow Washington's lead. President Nixon's July 25 announcement of a trip to mainland China stunned them, because it removed a cornerstone of their foreign policy and opened the government to a barrage of domestic attack.

In 1975 and 1982, senior planners worried about a similar quick-tilt by the United States toward the PLO, another actor that Washington had said it would never recognize. According to one high-ranking official:

> Kissinger was a very powerful [policymaker]. And as such, he put us in a very difficult position. His trip to China [on July 9, 1971] placed us in an entirely new situation. And we felt that this might happen again on [U.S. policy toward] the PLO. If it does, it will have repercussions throughout Japan. The prime minister and foreign minister would be asked what in the world they have been doing. We would naturally be the target of such criticism. . . . The public, [political] parties, newspapers—everyone would be after us.[9]

As for the Washington statements on PLO nonrecognition, this source continued:

> The United States has said that it will have nothing to do with Arafat . . . with the PLO. We find this hard to believe . . . [for] in the 1970s we heard rumors about U.S. talks with the PLO. And today [in 1981] we see such press reports as [the *Los Angeles Times*] story [of July 5, 1981] indicating a history of U.S.-PLO contact since 1974. Not all of these stories and rumors may be true. But we feel that some of them are.[10]

Thus, in early 1975, Miki favored informal ties to the PLO largely for reasons of long-term need. At the same time, however, he realized that the extent of contact would be restricted by several more-immediate considerations. In his view, the government was clearly "not in a position to recognize [the PLO] diplomatically as a nation."

For Miki, the PLO was simply not a nation. Although the organization may have had a population, it lacked a homeland and a basic set of laws that would satisfy the requirements of international legal recognition. More to the point, a full-fledged relationship with the PLO might light a short fuse in Washington. Something less, the prime minister felt, would not collide with any tenets of U.S. foreign policy. As he explained: "We would not have to bring up the matter [of the PLO office] in our talks with Washington, as long as we did not establish diplomatic relations with the PLO."[11]

Finally, the prime minister appears to have shared Foreign Ministry concern over the fluid state of Persian Gulf affairs. Since the early 1970s, policy planners in the Middle East Bureau had readily acknowledged the importance of the PLO as a representative of the Palestinian people, but they were uncertain whether it was the only such group. In their judgment, Japan should adopt a wait-and-see policy until the lines between representative and represented became more clearly drawn. Failure to exercise caution, Middle East Bureau officials believed, could lead to open embrace of an entity that might later be out of power or at odds with another organization, vying for power. As one bureau member remarked:

> The Japanese government is not in a position to decide . . . what particular group of Palestinians is the only representative of the whole people . . . because we don't know this. There may be some other representatives. We know for a fact that the PLO is the most influential and largest body representing the Palestinian people. That is for certain. But we don't know whether they are the only representatives. . . . It is a political stand.[12]

Having signaled his decisions on an office and nonrecognition, the prime minister waited for a reply from the PLO. He was not disappointed. In Beirut, PLO Chairman Yassir Arafat and other leaders welcomed Miki's statement. From the early 1970s they had used the Arab embassies in Tokyo "to float trial balloons on an information center in Japan." For them, the prime minister's proposal seemed to suggest that something better might be in the offing.

From the PLO's perspective, an office would establish ties to the non-Arab nations most able to help a future Palestinian state. Arafat and others felt that a new homeland would have to look to Japan as a model for development. The trend of less-developed countries, they judged, had been to rely, ill-advisedly, on the U.S. or Soviet experience. The result, in most cases, appeared to be economic weakness that undercut political autonomy. As one PLO official remarked:

> The newly developed countries have used two main methods of mod-

ernization—the so-called Western one and the Eastern-Soviet one.
Those who copied the Americans faced many, many problems . . .
as we have seen in Iran under the Shah. Those who copied the Soviet
one have faced the same problems. Such a state, one that lacks a
deep-rooted economy, means nothing. It is not a state . . . [since] it
is not politically independent.[13]

For the PLO, Japan was different. The Japanese economic system
was neither Western nor Soviet; moreover, it had been successful. "You
can see this," the same PLO source related, "in the Japanese invasion
of the U.S. market. America's productivity is declining . . . [and] the
Americans are simply unable to compete with the Japanese."[14]

This view of Japan as a mentor for modernization and a possible
donor of aid moved Arafat to favor Miki's offer. The result was the
start that spring of talks on the terms of a PLO residence in Japan.
The issues raised during the next year became a mirror of sorts, reflecting the common interest in Middle East peace that drew the two
sides together and the reverse images of diplomatic difference and
occasional mistrust that tended to pull them apart.

In a series of secret communications, PLO leaders first pressed
Tokyo on a matter it did not care to discuss. Through the Arab embassies in Japan and a personal envoy sent in June, Yassir Arafat argued
for diplomatic recognition by the government. The reason for this request evidently stemmed from the PLO chairman's assessment of U.S.
policy in the Middle East. During an interview with the Japanese press
on July 13, 1975, he noted American hostility toward the PLO, citing
Washington's refusal to invite the organization to the Geneva Conference and what he termed "unlimited U.S. arms to Israel."[15] Arafat
may have calculated that diplomatic relations with Japan, a U.S. ally,
could symbolically counter America's effort to "isolate the PLO."

Tokyo's response to this demand was a resounding no. Clearly, the
constraints behind the prime minister's statement of February 5 still
remained. As far as Miki was concerned, the government's position on
nonrecognition was nonnegotiable.

Unwilling to relent just yet, the PLO employed two new tactics
against Japan. On July 13 and 24 Chairman Arafat and Political Director
Farouk al-Kaddoumi publicly criticized the Japanese government, reiterating their dissatisfaction with Tokyo's attitude toward the Palestinian
people. Nevertheless, Arafat and Kaddoumi were careful not to end
the dialogue and, instead, offered Japan a way to show its good faith
toward them. According to both men, Tokyo should formally invite a
PLO delegation to discuss diplomatic privilege and other matters per-
taining to the diplomatic mission in Japan.

The Japanese government again refused. Because a formal invitation would imply recognition, the prime minister used unofficial channels to invite the organization for talks about an office. Arafat accepted, and on August 14, his representative, Shafiq Hout, met LDP party Secretary Yasuhiro Nakasone, Foreign Minister Kiichi Miyazawa, and members of the Foreign Ministry Middle East Bureau. During those sessions, government officials emphasized that concessions on diplomatic recognition and diplomatic privilege would not be forthcoming. Still, they hoped that a residence could be treated like a diplomatic mission in every other respect.[16] Expressing neither satisfaction nor dissatisfaction, Hout made the organization's first formal request for an office in Tokyo. For Japanese leaders, a basic understanding had been achieved on the nature of the relationship. The discussions could therefore turn to the finer details of an office arrangement.

To prepare for this new round of bargaining, Miki asked Middle East Bureau Director Teruhiko Nakamura to construct a set of core positions for the government. In the judgment of Nakamura and his bureau assistants, Tokyo first had a major policy dilemma on its hands. For diplomatic and political reasons, the government could not grant diplomatic status to the office. Yet, for diplomatic and political reasons, the government could not allow an office unless its personnel followed the customary rules of diplomatic behavior. The need to have it both ways became apparent on the matter of international terrorism. "Under international law," one official related, "no embassy engages in international terrorism or encourages or assists others [to do so] . . . [and] in the case of the PLO office, we were not certain whether this fell under international law."[17]

Alarm over this issue sprang from the highly publicized activities of the Japanese Red Army. In May 1972, three members of that organization, armed with automatic rifles and hand grenades, attacked a crowd of people at Lod International Airport near Tel Aviv, killing twenty-five and wounding seventy-two. Two years later, in September 1974, another three terrorists entered the French embassy in the Hague, where they held the ambassador and eight others hostage. After obtaining the release of a fellow terrorist from French prison and $300,000 in ransom, the three departed for Damascus, where they turned themselves into the PLO. The following August, the Red Army struck again. In Kuala Lumpur, five terrorists seized the U.S. consul and eight others, demanding freedom for five Red Army members who were in Japanese prison. Again they succeeded, and on August 5, ten terrorists flew to Tripoli for political asylum.

What concerned Japanese officials in late 1975 were field reports and other intelligence sources suggesting a direct link between the Red Army and the PLO. In Tokyo, however, Nakamura and his assistants could not independently verify whether such a relationship existed. To be on the safe side, they concluded that Japan would have to make two demands of the PLO. The government would need, first, a statement from the organization denouncing terrorist activities of all kinds and, more important, the promise that office personnel would not meet members of the Red Army or ultraradical groups in Japan. Explaining these stipulations, a source related:

> We wanted an agreement that [PLO office personnel] would not have anything to do with violent radicals while they were in Japan. It was on this condition that we recognized the [PLO's] right to enter and exit Japan. This is still the case. Whenever friends of the PLO come to Japan, we permit these visits on this condition. And when we agreed to the office, we made it clear that . . . noncontact with Japanese ultraradicals in Japan . . . along with a disavowal of any relationship with terrorist activities . . . would be stipulations for the establishment of an office.[18]

Another concern for Nakamura and his assistants centered on diplomatic discretion. To them, informal rules of etiquette dictated that embassies refrain from disagreeing publicly with the foreign policies of their host country. Again, however, the PLO office might fall outside the parameters of normal diplomatic behavior. Tokyo planners thus appeared to worry that an airing of differences not only would embarrass the government but also would strain relations with the Saudis and other Arab advocates of Japan-PLO ties. To prevent office outbursts and diplomatic explosion, Nakamura and his assistants decided to require that "office personnel not openly criticize Japan's foreign policy [in Japan]."[19]

Besides these two demands, the Middle East Bureau wanted to raise a third, more central issue—the question of mutal recognition between Israel and the PLO. Clearly, Nakamura, his superiors, and his subordinates did not expect any concessions from the organization. Nevertheless, they felt obliged to impress upon PLO leaders that all Palestinians could not live in peace until the two adversaries first agreed to do so.

Nakamura and his assistants then considered what proposal would elicit Arafat's acceptance of the office conditions and consideration of mutual recognition. In their judgment, reassurances regarding the powers of the PLO man in Japan might do the trick. Although the government could not deal with the Tokyo representative as a diplomat, it could give him the right "to come to the foreign ministry and talk to [Japanese] officials just like any other embassy person."

With these positions and inducement in hand, Nakamura and his emissaries met their PLO counterparts in Tokyo, New York, and Beirut. During those sessions, Hout, Kaddoumi, and other representatives came armed with their own demands. Having yielded earlier on diplomatic privilege, they now wanted guarantees on entry and exit, police protection, and other items that would enable their agent to function effectively in Japan. In addition, PLO officials made a request that would add prestige to the office arrangement. According to them, the government should issue an official statement of international support for the Palestinian cause. Apparently to induce acceptance, they also mentioned something that Tokyo wanted to hear. During the talks, Arafat's men reiterated that they personally favored the right of Israel to exist within its recognized borders.[20]

The bureau decided to say yes to both demands, but for two entirely different reasons. Nakamura and his assistants evidently viewed the matter of office guarantees as a straightforward quid pro quo. Tokyo would gladly accept if the PLO reciprocated on the conditions regarding international terrorism and foreign policy criticism.

The assessment of the second demand, however, was a bit more complex. Nakamura and his assistants were leery, at first, of the personal leanings on mutual recognition. Though judging that these statements accurately reflected sentiment within the Fatah/Arafat wing of the PLO, bureau members believed that opposition by "guerilla elements committed to the destruction of Israel" had prevented the PLO chairman from espousing a formal position. Should Arafat make this statement publicly, one official quipped, "he might become the victim of a sort of internal terrorism." For this reason, bureau officials felt, the organization had been unable to formulate "a more unified position" on Israel and mutual recogniton.[21]

This perception of PLO policy disarray notwithstanding, Nakamura and his assistants concluded that Japan should support the Palestinian cause since, in their view, the government had nothing to lose. Such an announcement, the bureau judged, would merely articulate what they already felt. In that sense, "it was hardly a concession."

During talks with the PLO, Japanese representatives said their government would back "the legitimate right of self-determination for Palestinian people" and then specified how Japan would interpret this phrase. According to them, the word *legitimate* was the key. As one official explained:

> For us, "legitimate" included the right for an independent state. From the Palestinian viewpoint, they had been thrown out of their homeland and wanted help in getting it back. This became the "legitimate right of self-determination." . . . As long as the Palestinians are denied a state, they will continue to be a cause of unrest throughout the Middle

East. . . . This is what we believed needed to be done to secure peace
[in the region]. . . . And as a result of the [office] negotiators, we
agreed that an independent state should be recognized if it is
established.[22]

Japanese representatives stressed, however, that this alone would
not be enough. From the government's perspective, *legitimate* also meant
mutual agreement to live in peace. Therefore, the term would have to
imply PLO recognition of Israel's right to exist. As their response, PLO
negotiators welcomed the first interpretation and adopted official silence on the second.

After several months of probing and posturing, each side agreed
to accept the other's major demands. Then, apparently in late 1975,
the PLO made an additional request. Speaking on behalf of the organization, Kaddoumi asked for an invitation to meet the prime minister
and foreign minister for discussions about the office arrangement. The
Middle East Bureau had no objections to the PLO political director's
trip to Tokyo, but it opposed a formal invitation, which would imply
recognition. To sidestep this problem, the bureau and the prime minister's office decided to invite Kaddoumi as the guest of the Liberal-
Democratic Party for talks with party president Takeo Miki and other
party officers.

On April 21, 1976, the PLO political director visited the Foreign
Ministry. During his session there, Foreign Minister Kiichi Miyazawa
reminded Kaddoumi of Japan's dual support for UN Resolution 242
and the legitimate right of self-determination for the Palestinian people.
Miyazawa also lectured him on the need for direct dialogue between
Israel and the PLO to establish lasting peace in the region. Following
the foreign minister's comments, the new Middle East Bureau director,
Hideo Kagami, told Kaddoumi that the PLO could best promote friendship between the Japanese and Palestinian people by cutting its ties to
hijackings and other terrorists acts. The PLO political director then
spoke. While ignoring Miyazawa's proddings on mutual recognition,
he emphasized that the organization had no relationship with these
incidents and, indeed, favored diplomatic means to solve the problems
of the area.[23]

Five days later, Kaddoumi met Prime Minister Miki, who reaffirmed his support for Palestinian self-determination, Israeli withdrawal
from the occupied territories, and a military ceasefire in the Middle
East. After this visit and several delays, the PLO office eventually
opened for unofficial business on December 19, 1976.

The new relationship did not stop there, however. In late 1981, both Japan and the PLO moved toward a closer political union. The trigger for that movement was the burst of events surrounding the Camp David accords.

In November 1977, Egyptian President Anwar el-Sadat electrified the world when he announced his interest in traveling to Jerusalem and five days later spoke for peace before Israel's Knesset. During the next five months, the pace of diplomatic developments picked up. In January and February 1978, Presidents Carter and Sadat undertook historic visits to one another's capitals, and in April, Secretary of State Cyrus Vance indicated that the United States would start a new diplomatic push in the Persian Gulf area.

Senior officials in Tokyo were delighted. In their initial judgment, Washington would soon try to revive the Geneva peace process.[24] They were soon surprised. The dramatic negotiations among Carter, Begin, and Sadat in early September 1978 and the signing of "A Framework for Peace" on September 17 caused Tokyo hopes to soar. For ministry officials, an important first step had been taken. The document, a prelude to the Camp David accords, not only ended the state of war between Israel and the strongest Arab military power, but it also formalized Egypt's break from the Soviet Union in 1972 and raised the possibility of more U.S. aid to one of the weakest economies in the region.

Equally important, the agreement appeared to signify the start of a second step toward reconciliation between Israel and its Arab neighbors. In 1978, Japanese planners dismissed criticism by Arafat and the Gulf States of Sadat's trip to Israel and his talks with Carter and Begin. As one high-ranking official remarked: "They never say anything nice about anyone anyway." Indeed, from the foreign ministry's perpsective, Saudi Arabia, Jordan, and other Gulf State moderates might well support the trilateral initiative as the vehicle most able to end the conflict that most threatened their long-term interests. What followed was a clear disappointment.

Instead of abating, Arab attitudes hardened. In late March 1979, members of the Arab League met in Baghdad to consider sanctions against Egypt. Although Saudi Arabia and Jordan opposed Yassir Arafat's request for stiff economic measures against the United States, they agreed to back other demands, including the suspension of Cairo's membership in the league and a boycott of Egyptian companies doing business with Israel.

This intransigence by the moderate participants, Foreign Ministry officials judged, resulted from the situation unfolding in Iran. To Tokyo planners, the unexpected fall of the shah on January 16, 1979, and the continued slide of Teheran into civil chaos had removed a lynchpin of security in the region. Because they felt strategically exposed, officials in Riyadh and other Arab capitals may have been unable to opt for the move that would boldly alter the diplomatic status quo. According to one source:

> Camp David could have been more successful without the revolution in Iran. With the Shah's Iran sound and intact, moderate Arab countries could have felt safer to support the American move. But without the Shah's Iran, Saudi Arabia and Jordan felt . . . more susceptible to criticism from other Arab countries. So had the Iranian Revolution not occurred, President Carter may have been able to persuade the Saudis and Jordanians to join.[25]

In 1979, Foreign Ministry officials also feared that stubbornness of another sort dimmed the future of the Camp David accords. During the September 1978 negotiations, Prime Minister Begin had promised to forge ahead on the issue of Palestinian autonomy. Yet, his policies in 1979 seemed to signal a different message. Ten days after the start of talks with Egypt and the United States on Arab self-rule, the Israeli cabinet voted on June 4 to establish a new settlement near the West Bank city of Nablus, a center for Palestinian nationalism. The next day, Defense Minister Ezer Weizman moved to implement the cabinet decision, requisitioning two hundred acres of Arab-owned land for fifty Israeli families.

In Tokyo, three actions sparked skepticism about Begin's willingness to return any Palestinian land to Palestinian rule. More worrisome for the Japanese, however, was the chance that such actions might delegitimize the peace process throughout the Arab world.

Concerned that the Camp David agreement was slipping away, Tokyo tried to tighten its grip on friendship with the PLO. In early February 1980, Ryohei Murata, Japan's ambassador to the United Arab Emirates, met twice with a representative of Yassir Arafat. During those sessions, Arafat's man mentioned the chairman's interest in visiting Japan. Murata soon conveyed this message to the Foreign Ministry. Evidently after discussing the matter with Prime Minister Masayoshi Ohira and Foreign Minister Saburo Okita, Middle East Bureau Director Kanzuo Chiba asked Toshio Kimura if he would invite Arafat to Japan.

Kimura seemed to be an ideal choice. He had the diplomatic experience of a former foreign minister, and, more important, he had headed the Japan-Palestine Friendship Commission—a group of Diet members who favored closer contact with the PLO and the Gulf States.

As president of that organization, Kimura could extend a private invitation that would not signify diplomatic recognition by the government.

The former foreign minister decided to comply with Chiba's request. He shared Tokyo's disenchantment with the Camp David accords, feeling that "you cannot achieve real peace in the Middle East unless you solve the Palestinian issue." He was also more openly critical of the Carter administration, however, whose positions appeared "to put the cart before the horse." In Kimura's opinion, Washington had applied a laissez-faire policy regarding Begin and the issue of Palestinian territories. Equally disturbing, it had refused to support self-determination or a homeland for the Palestinian people.[26]

American inaction, Kimura believed, flowed from "the assumption in Washington that the PLO is only a guerilla organization . . . which cannot be dealt with as a party concerned with peace." Although conceding that these measures might protect Israel in the short run, he concluded that they would make Israel more intractable and make much-needed moderate Arab support more unlikely in the long run. In this sense, Carter's policies only promised to undercut U.S. influence and the U.S. peace effort in the Middle East. Kimura thus felt that Japan should build an independent network of ties that would independently protect Japan's interests in the Gulf area. For him, the invitation to Arafat would be an integral part of that strategy.[27]

Accordingly, in February 1980, Kimura sent invitations to Arafat and Kaddoumi through Ambassador Murata. To be consistent with Tokyo's position, he informed them that diplomatic recognition could not be claimed or inferred from this nongovernmental offer. At first, Arafat accepted Kimura's terms, but several weeks later he reversed his position.

In early March, Valéry Giscard d'Estaing toured the Middle East. During his eleven-day trip, the French president proclaimed his support for Palestinian rights and for PLO participation in the peace process. Moreover, he indicated his interest in inviting Arafat to Paris on an unofficial basis that would not confer diplomatic status to the PLO. For his purposes, though, Arafat evidently informed Kimura of Giscard's official invitation and, trying to use that misrepresentation as leverage, demanded that Tokyo extend the same courtesy to him. When Kimura declined, Arafat threatened to put the commission's invitation "in deep freeze." The bluff did not succeed, however, for Tokyo remained silent and Arafat stayed in Beirut.

Six months later, however, the roles of initiator and respondent suddenly switched, with Arafat asking for an invitation and the Japanese replying yes. The reason was an unexpected event that led to a change of PLO heart. In late September, military units of Iran and Iraq ex-

changed artillery and rocket fire near the major ports of Khorramshahr, Abadan, and Basra and soon clashed head-on along their border, with the fighting heaviest near the Shatt-al-Arab waterway. The violence quickly escalated when Iraq struck the oil refinery at Abadan; Iran then hit Baghdad, oil installations in two cities, and the petrochemical complex at Basra.

For Arafat, nothing could have been worse. First, the conflict shifted world attention away from Palestinian rights to new concerns about oil production in the two countries and tanker passage through the Strait of Hormuz to the south of Iran. Equally disturbing, the war was threatening to tear the Arab world apart.[28]

Throughout the fall, each of the Gulf States announced support for one of the two combatants. In early October, Jordan directly backed Iraq by providing vehicles to transport food and supplies to Baghdad army units. Several weeks later, Libyan leader Muammar el-Qaddafi reacted. He sent messages to King Khalid of Saudi Arabia and other Gulf leaders declaring his support for Teheran and urging them to align with the Moslems of Iran as a matter of "Islamic duty." The Saudis soon sent Qaddafi a message of their own. In late October, Riyadh broke relations with Tripoli.

In Beirut, Arafat and other organization leaders feared that this division might unravel the united front behind the PLO. Faced with a deteriorating situation, Arafat and other PLO leaders began to reconsider the invitation from Kimura. In their view, a highly publicized trip to Japan might regain lost ground by reawakening international interest in Palestinian rights and regrouping their allies in the Gulf area.

In early October, they made their move. Under instructions from the organization, PLO Tokyo Representative Fathi Abdul Hamid asked Kimura to visit his office on October 11. Ostensibly, the two men would discuss an invitation to the mid-December meeting of the Palestinian National Council (PNC) in Damascus. In reality, both sides knew that much more was at stake, for nine days earlier Hamid and Middle East Bureau Director Ryohei Murata had met in Tokyo.

During that session on October 2, the PLO representative mentioned that the PNC wished to have Kimura attend its proceedings as a guest discussant. Hamid also raised the possibility of a meeting between Kimura and Arafat and then pressed Tokyo on the item that he wanted most—diplomatic recognition of the PLO chairman's trip to Japan. Hamid did this implicitly by chastising Japan for its poor record on Palestinian rights. According to the PLO representative, Tokyo's support for UN Resolution 242 was not enough; a better-faith effort was clearly needed.

As he related:

Japan says that both parties [Israel and the PLO] should mutually recognize each other. Now, from our point of view, who gave Japan this right to advise us on this question? . . . In order to play a role, you should be neutral with the two parties. [But] Japan is not neutral. Japan recognizes Israel . . . has diplomatic relations with Israel, while having nothing with the PLO. From our side, we are not going to give Japanese advice any consideration, any importance because it is a repetition of U.S. policy. However, if Japan recognizes the two parties, then it can play a role. This is the question for the Japanese government: when is it going to be neutral?[29]

After Hamid's tirade, Murata left to discuss the matter with Foreign Minister Masayoshi Ito and Chief Cabinet Secretary Kiichi Miyazawa. Evidently, their initial reaction to the PLO representative's demand was a collective groan. In the words of one Foreign Ministry official:

Mr. Hamid still has difficulty understanding that we are not going to recognize the PLO. . . . In spite of his efforts, we still feel no pressure on this issue . . . [because] there is absolutely no need to recognize the PLO.[30]

With their policy on nonrecognition undiminished, Ito and Miyazawa gave the go-ahead signal for Kimura's trip. As key foreign policymakers in the Suzuki cabinet, the two men agreed with the Middle East Bureau assessment that "progress toward comprehensive peace under the Camp David accords [had been] most disappointing . . . and that efforts should be made to turn CDA into a wider, broader arrangement so that it would not be . . . just a bilateral agreement between Egypt and Israel.[31]

On October 6, Ito echoed these sentiments during a discussion with former Secretary of State Cyrus Vance. In diplomatic language, the foreign minister praised the Camp David agreement "as a necessary first step toward peace" in the region and added that a second step, leading to Israeli-PLO agreement on coexistence must be taken. Otherwise, violence between the two parties would persist well into the future. The former secretary of state supported Ito's position but cautioned that the U.S. presidential election in November and the Israeli parliamentary contest the following fall would momentarily block any activity on Middle East peace.[32]

What concerned Ito, Miyazawa, and Middle East Bureau members, however, was the future of the Camp David accords after that. Taking a long-range view, they judged that Japan should rekindle contact with three influential forces, calling for policy change in the United States and Israel. They apparently judged that a diplomacy of informal alignments would help build pressure for future movement in the peace process.

In Tokyo, the European Economic Community (EEC) was the first actor to receive leadership attention. On June 13, 1980, the ten members of the EEC had met in Vienna to issue an eleven-point statement on "a framework for a comprehensive settlement in the Middle East." While reaffirming the EEC's commitment to the security of Israel, the document called for "the recognition of the rights of the Palestinian people" and termed the PLO a party "which will have to be associated with the negotiations."

The foreign minister at the time, Saburo Okita, and members of the Middle East Bureau had decided to support the statement, since the thinking of Japan and Western Europe coincided regarding the Camp David peace process. Not only did Tokyo and the EEC assume that lasting peace required a broad-based solution on Palestinian rights, but they also feared that anything less would drive radical Arab elements to use greater violence against Israel.[33]

Under both Okita and Ito, the Foreign Ministry hoped that the Tokyo-EEC alliance would persuade elite opinion in America and Israel of the need for a comprehensive settlement. As one official emphasized:

> The whole thing [the EEC movement] is a mechanism to induce . . . to invite more concessions from Israel and the PLO. Neither the EEC countries nor Japan can play a principal role. [Nevertheless] whatever we say is from the hope or conviction that this might help the Israeli people and the PLO make more concessions and enter into negotiations. But so far U.S. administrations and Israel have wanted to have moderate representatives of the Palestinian people join them, and avoid talking to the PLO in the belief that they can continue to ignore this group of terrorists. The Europeans and Japanese feel that they [the United States and Israel] cannot keep ignoring the PLO. It is more constructive to invite them to join the talks. Of course, [this would be] on the condition that they recognize the right of Israel to exist.[34]

When Ito met Western European heads of state in December, he reiterated Tokyo's interest in working together on "the challenges to world peace." For the next half-year, the foreign minister and other Japanese leaders believed that uncertainties about Reagan's Middle East policy and Israel's election would force a lull in Tokyo-EEC diplomacy. Nevertheless, they remained confident that the basis had been laid for their new multilateral effort.

Parallel to this was a new thrust toward "a very important country in the Arab world." From 1979, planners in the Middle East Bureau had wanted the foreign minister to visit Cairo as a way of shoring up ties to that capital. The time for such a trip did not appear to be ripe, however. The Arab League's decision to boycott Egypt in March 1979 fueled Tokyo's anxiety about the reprisals that might follow a visit. The Iran-Iraq war eventually changed that assessment, however. For the Middle East Bureau, the widening split among the Arab countries meant that the foreign minister could travel to Cairo with minimal damage to Japan–Gulf State ties. As a result, the bureau recommended that Ito go to commemorate the first phase of Tokyo-financed work on the Suez Canal.[35]

The foreign minister agreed and, on December 17, met for ninety minutes with the Egyptian head of state. During that session, Sadat first thanked Japan for assistance on the Ismailia stretch of canal construction and then accepted a "letter of friendship" as well as an invitation from Prime Minister Zenko Suzuki to visit Japan as the official guest of the government.[36]

The Egyptian president next turned to the issue that was most on his mind. He reiterated his optimism that President-elect Reagan would move forward on the Camp David peace process and mentioned his plan to send Vice-President Hosni Mubarak to the United States for consultations with the new administration. Sadat's mood then shifted as he reviewed the Palestinian problem. While thanking Japan for its international support, he wondered aloud whether Tokyo and the EEC might help shape U.S. thinking on this matter. As he emphasized, only the United States had great influence with Israel.

The Japanese foreign minister responded indirectly, stating his belief that the future of the Camp David accords hinged on the outcome of mutual recognition and Palestinian self-determination. Sadat agreed and ended the discussion by criticizing the PLO and stressing the need to expand the peace process, perhaps with the participation of Jordan.

After returning to Tokyo, Ito resumed work with Kiichi Miyazawa, the Middle East Bureau, and Toshio Kimura on the third prop of Japan's Middle Eastern peace diplomacy—the Arafat trip to Japan. The issues before the government and Kimura flowed from his meeting with the PLO leader in mid-December.

On December 13, Kimura arrived at the PNC convention. Evidently, the "guest discussant" first wanted to guage the depth of the PLO chairman's interest in visiting Japan. Having been rebuffed earlier in the year, the former foreign minister was in no mood to be slighted again. During the PNC proceedings, he was approached by several moderate participants who urged him to raise the possibility of another invitation with their chairman. Showing some emotion, Kimura snapped that Arafat already had an invitation before him; therefore, any initiative would have to be taken by the PLO leader himself.[37]

When the two men met that evening, Kimura started the discussion with a pointed remark. He commented that the PLO would have to stop its policies of contempt and hostility toward Israel. At some time, he said, it would have to recognize the right of Israel to exist. Arafat replied that "he was thinking along those lines" and reassured Kimura that "PLO opinion had changed." According to the chairman, the PLO had once felt that way, but now he had no intention of destroying Israel.[38]

As president of the Japan-Palestine Friendship Commission, Kimura then turned the bargaining screws. He stated bluntly that the Iran-Iraq war had undermined Arab unity and had removed the Palestinian issue from world attention. The former foreign minister next reminded Arafat of his prior insistence on an official invitation from the Japanese government.

The chairman replied: "You understand our situation. We are in a very difficult position and for that reason I would very much like to visit Japan." Arafat then dropped his earlier demand, saying that he would, "in principle," accept the offer of the Japan-Palestine Friendship Commission. The chairman added, however, that he wished to have some guarantee on meetings with the prime minister and foreign minister while in Japan.[39]

Kimura did not object, since Suzuki and Ito could welcome and meet Arafat without conferring diplomatic status on the PLO. To Kimura, the formula was a technical matter that could be settled after his return to Japan. For the moment, he was ecstatic. He had extracted Arafat's promise to visit Japan on terms favorable to the government. Nothing else was more important. As he related:

> The timing of our invitation was perfect. He [Arafat] was in a weak position and still wanted to come [to Japan] even though the invitation would be unofficial. The trip was clearly his overriding objective . . . [because of] the prestige that would be associated with it.[40]

When he returned to Tokyo, Kimura briefed Ito, Miyazawa, and the Middle East Bureau on his conversation with Arafat. The reaction was mixed. The officals were pleased by the chairman's acceptance, but they remained suspicious of Arafat's statements on Israel, concluding that "he may have said what he said because he was talking to private citizen Kimura, not to Prime Minister Suzuki." In 1980, officials continued to doubt whether a fragmented organization had been able to fashion a unified policy.

Despite this assessment, Ito and Miyazawa gave Kimura clearance to arrange the guarantee Arafat wanted. Before broaching the subject of a formula with PLO representative Hamid, Kimura judged that two possibilities—a formal invitation from the government and a personal letter from Prime Minister Suzuki—were out of the question. Under international law, either formula would indicate de facto recognition of the PLO. Following several sessions in February 1981, Kimura proposed to Hamid that he, as president of the Japan-Palestine Friendship Commission, send Arafat a letter confirming his earlier invitation and mentioning the prime minister's wish to discuss "the general problems of the Middle East" with the PLO chairman. It was in this way, Kimura explained, that "we saved their face."[41]

After receiving Hamid's approval, he drafted the letter and turned it over to the Foreign Ministry in early March. The written message was then sent to the Japanese embassy in Beirut for forwarding to a representative of the PLO.[42]

In April, Hamid left Tokyo for a PNC meeting in Damascus, where PLO leaders discussed the letter and invitation among themselves.[43] When he returned to Japan, Hamid informed Kimura that Arafat would accept and then pressured him for a June date.

Kimura discussed the request with the prime minister, the foreign minister, and the chief cabinet secretary. The four men agreed that the trip would have to be scheduled several months later. During the spring of 1981, Tokyo's planning for an Arafat visit became known in the United States. As its response, the State Department sent the Japanese embassy in Washington several mild warnings on the potential for adverse reaction in the Congress and damage to the bilateral relationship.

Although these communications did not sidetrack the trip, they apparently reminded Suzuki, Ito, Miyazawa, Kimura, and the Middle East Bureau just how sensitive Washington opinion could be. In their estimate, a June date would give American critics enough political ammunition to fire at Japan. According to Kimura:

> I spoke to Prime Minister Suzuki, the chief cabinet secretary and foreign minister. We thought it would be inappropriate to have Arafat visit [in June] after Suzuki's trip [in May] to North America. . . . Reagan would certainly criticize our Mideast policy, saying that he didn't understand what in the world we were trying to do. . . . We also decided to forgo it [a June visit] because it would occur before the economic conference in Ottawa [set for July]. It might put Reagan at odds with Western Europe over its policy toward the Middle East. . . . Japan would of course be in the same position. We therefore felt it best to have Arafat come to Japan after things settled down. To have Arafat visit us before then would have been too traumatic for Reagan.[44]

Kimura accordingly told Hamid that June was "inconvenient" and suggested that October might be better. The Tokyo PLO representative and PLO leaders in Beirut reacted with strong displeasure, reiterating the chairman's desire to visit Japan as soon as possible. August, they countered, would be fine.

Kimura and the government again demurred, since Begin and Sadat were expected to meet Reagan separately in the United States in August. The Japanese felt that a Suzuki-Arafat encounter in August would help the PLO upstage those talks and would incur Washington's wrath. As a consequence, August also became "inconvenient."[45]

When informed of this decision, PLO leaders fumed over Tokyo's intransigence. Despite their unhappiness, however, they did not decline the commission's invitation. In Tokyo, Kimura and government officials quietly hoped that they would not decline. From their perspective, recent developments made a trip even more vital.

For his part, Kimura reached this conclusion through an assessment of U.S. factors. The former foreign minister felt that the new administration had picked up the bad diplomatic habits of its predecessor. In line with the Carter White House, President Reagan and his advisors had adopted a Middle East approach characterized by total support for Israel and total opposition to the PLO. In Kimura's opinion, an example of the former was Reagan's response to Israeli air strikes against the Iraqi nuclear reactor in June and to the attack on a PLO office in a heavily populated part of Beirut in July. Sending Special Ambassador Philip Habib to Israel, Kimura felt, was not enough. Stronger action should have been taken, including the postponement of advanced jet fighter transfers, for "anything less would inflame Arab suspicions of America and further isolate it in the Gulf area."[46]

Regarding U.S. policy on the PLO, Kimura believed that the Reagan/Haig emphasis on East-West confrontation had preempted support for Palestinian rights. In his view, Washington's concern over terrorist activity by the PLO and Soviet influence within that organization had spurred a strident, anti-Arafat attitude. Kimura worried that such a stance, rather than containing Soviet influence, would push Arafat and other PLO leaders into the Soviet camp, thus strengthening Moscow's hand throughout the Middle East. The result would be a more polarized Persian Gulf region, with no middle ground on which to build lasting peace.

Besides these considerations, Kimura had another new reason for dealing directly with Arafat and the PLO. On April 28, U.S. Defense Secretary Caspar Weinberger, in a San Francisco speech, had argued vehemently for a stronger defense posture by Japan. Kimura believed that such demands emanated from the situation in the Middle East.

Throughout 1979 and 1980, the United States continued to break off large chunks of its Seventh Fleet for operations in the Indian Ocean and the Persian Gulf. Although the swing of naval forces helped the United States deal with the hostage crisis in Iran and the Soviet move into Afghanistan, it left the United States numerically disadvantaged against a growing Soviet naval presence in the Western Pacific. Kimura feared that future instability in the Middle East would make Japan not only more insecure at home but also more vulnerable to unwise calls for massive rearmament from abroad. For Kimura, "there was [thus] no such thing as a purely Middle Eastern problem."

Senior decision makers in Tokyo agreed in part with Kimura's analysis, judging it to be "unfair for President Reagen to refuse to deal with the PLO just because they are terrorists." "After all," one official commented, "Prime Minister Begin himself was reputed to have been quite a terrorist."[47]

In addition, Ito, Miyazawa, and members of the Middle East Bureau were disturbed about Israel's decision of June 30 to annex Arab East Jerusalem and make it part of the de facto capital. In their view, this "continuation of Begin's unproductive policies [will] allow Arab countries to claim that Camp David [was] nothing more than a device to cloak Israel's neverending occupation of Palestinian territories."

Despite this assessment, the Japanese government had one reason for hope. The expected victory by Israel's Labour Party in the parliamentary contest in July might bring to power a new prime minister, committed to a more flexible response on the Palestinian issue.

The official tally of the July 6 election made Japanese officials most unhappy. After fighting off the charge of Shimon Perez, Begin's Likud bloc was left with forty-eight seats and the Labour Party with forty-seven. To raise his total to the sixty-one seats needed for a majority, the prime minister struck bargains with leaders of the National Religious Party, Agudath Israel, and Tami.

Japanese officials regarded this as the worst possible outcome, for they believed that even a strong Begin government would have been preferable to a weak Begin government. Indebted to conservative religious parties and facing a strong Labour opposition, the reelected prime minister could not be expected to make the compromises necessary for a settlement of the Palestinian issue. Thus, the political deadlock between Israel and the PLO would have to be broken by the PLO.

It was in this context that Japan's decision makers began to reevaluate the PLO chairman's visit to Japan. Because of electoral parity in Jerusalem, senior planners in Tokyo began to regard the trip as a way of educating Arafat on the need for reconciliation with Israel. Clearly, the Japanese believed that they could not press him directly on an initiative during his stay. Still, they felt they could show the chairman the benefits that might flow from a moderate policy toward Israel. In their estimate:

> It [was] important for Arafat to come to Japan and see what Japan is like for himself. . . . Then we hope that he may, that he will increase his understanding of Japan . . . [its] importance in the Middle East . . . and what a more conciliatory posture on mutual recognition will mean for the PLO.[48]

For the moment, Tokyo officials realized that internal differences within the PLO would prevent a quick shift of organization policy. Taking a long-range view, however, they hoped that the chairman's visit to industrial Japan would eventually persuade him and the PLO to take the desired diplomatic path. As one official remarked:

> Suppose Mr. Arafat goes to some session of the United Nations . . . and makes public a new PLO stand vis-à-vis Israel . . . denouncing this long-held aim of extinguishing Israel. Now, he says that the Palestinian people and the PLO recognize the existence of Israel . . . [and] the right of the Israeli people to live in secure and recognized boundaries. And that they recognize Israel as a partner in negotiations for peace and renounce, at least for the time being, any resort to force against Israel. I think this will appeal tremendously to public opinion in the United States . . . as well as to world opinion. Then that will turn into strong pressure on the Israeli government. That is our hope. If Mr. Arafat and the PLO change themselves in this way . . . President Reagan will no longer be able to dismiss them as a group of terrorists.[49]

After July 1981, the Japanese position on the Middle East seemed to be set. Although they again deflected Arafat's demands for diplomatic recognition, senior officials grew confident that the PLO chairman would come in October and would be followed by Sadat in November. Then the unexpected happened.

On October 6, the Egyptian leader was assassinated. At first, uncertainty about Cairo's stability permeated the Japanese government. Soon, however, this anxiety was somewhat alleviated by the president-apparent and his presumed policy line. On October 10, the day of Sadat's funeral, Hosni Mubarak met privately with Foreign Minister Sunao Sonoda. During that session, the Egyptian vice-president stated his intention to stand firmly behind the Camp David accords. Moreover, he displayed "a conservative personality . . . [which suggested] that a major shift in diplomacy would not occur overnight."[50]

Thus, for the moment, it appeared that Cairo's long-term view of a comprehensive peace would stay unchanged. Nevertheless, the death of Sadat raised several thorny issues for the Japanese. Following the assassination, one source explained, "Arafat made this statement glorifying the murder. . . . That created a big problem for us. . . . This may sound a bit ghoulish, but in Japan it is commonly said that you don't practice witchcraft on the dead."[51]

In the Foreign Ministry, senior officials were beseiged by LDP members of the Diet, who both admired Sadat and questioned the propriety of inviting such an individual as the PLO chairman. Despite this pressure and their own repulsion to Arafat's statement, Tokyo decision makers believed that the trip would have to go through. "Cancellation at this stage," they judged, "would be a large minus" for Japan's position in the Middle East.[52] As a result, they explained to the legislators what was at stake and what the loss would be, eventually prodding acceptance of the welcome that had already been prepared.

In addition to internal resistance, ministry planners had to contend with a more delicate external constraint—from the United States. Not wanting to "surprise Washington," they informed the Reagan administration of the details of the forthcoming visit and of what they hoped to accomplish. The reaction was less than enthusiastic, but that, in the ministry's view, was expected.

As one source observed:

> The U.S. government has [consistently] told us not to do or say anything with regard to Mideast peace, arguing the [such statements or actions] would put it in a difficult position. Certainly, we feel that the role Japan can play is quite limited, and that America . . . not Israel . . . holds the key to Mideast peace. We would of course be happy to leave this problem to America if, apart from a few minor differences, we judged U.S. policy to be correct. But we feel that U.S. policy is incorrect. . . . And so we are at a loss, when told to do nothing about a region that is so crucial for Japan.[53]

This difference of opinion notwithstanding, the Japanese wished to avoid any incidents during the Arafat visit that might further upset Washington. Accordingly, they sent the PLO chairman, through Kimura, four conditions whose acceptance was nonnegotiable. First, Arafat would have to reconfirm his understanding that diplomatic status for the PLO office in Tokyo could neither be demanded nor granted while he was in Japan. Second, he must sidestep any criticism of Sadat. Third, Arafat would have to refrain from making any speeches or propaganda-laden statements after arriving at Haneda Airport. Finally, the PLO delegation would have to disarm itself, leaving all weapons behind at the airport.

Evidently to the surprise of ministry officials, Arafat accepted these demands with little quibbling. He agreed to the first condition, saying that "it would present no problems." Moreover, he raised eyebrows in Tokyo with his praise for Sadat, "his close friend of the past thirty years." Arafat also discarded the speech he had intended to deliver at the airport. Finally, after some complaining, he agreed to have his delegation enter Japan weapons-free.

This quick acceptance, and the subsequent meeting between Arafat and Suzuki, suggested that something more than the Iran-Iraq War was now on the chairman's mind. In that discussion of October 14, Arafat spoke bitterly of America's refusal to deal directly with him, while repeating "his big wish for a dialogue with . . . [and] for diplomatic relations with the United States."[54]

In hindsight, it appears that the surprise reelection of an Israeli who was dead set against his organization forced Arafat to reshuffle his objectives. Initially, ministry planners suspected that the chairman had looked first, in 1980, to France and perhaps to Italy for an official visit that might sway U.S. public opinion. Unfortunately for him, neither country was prepared to extend a welcome on a government-to-government basis. With the European channel thus closed, and with Begin still in power, he may have turned to Japan as his only way of influencing Washington—as the one actor who could change what then appeared to be a long-term anti-PLO status quo.

Naturally, Tokyo continued to disclaim any diplomatic implications from the trip, but it had at least assured him of meetings with the prime minister and the foreign minister during his stay. To Arafat, that may have been enough. He could, of course, falsely claim the equivalent of official recognition. More to the point, though, he could use Japanese leaders to convey a second message to the American government.

In staff-level talks, members of al-Fatah told Foreign Ministry planners of their support for the Fahd plan, which implicitly recognized Israel's right to exist. In his own conversation with Suzuki, Arafat also said: "We are prepared to live in peace with Israel." Then he added a caveat:

It is difficult for us to make this our formal position right now. We would do so, if there was a possibility that Israel would reciprocate by recognizing the PLO or the right of Palestinian self-determination. But that will not happen . . . [and] so we would in effect tear up our final card by playing it at this moment.[55]

Given the thrust of these remarks, Arafat seemed to be telling U.S. leaders that Middle East peace could be had—for a political price. The U.S. government must eventually accept and support the PLO as an equal partner; otherwise, Israel and the PLO would forever stay at arms length. It was thus up to Washington to break the impasse and form the trilateral bond on which a negotiated settlement would have to rest.

After Arafat's departure on October 15, Japanese planners transmitted the contents of his conversation with Suzuki to the Reagan administration. Eight months later, however, it became evident that the signal had failed to impress Washington. On July 6, 1982, Israeli forces encircled Moslem West Beirut, sealing off PLO forces from outside support. Following five weeks of strike and counterstrike, Arafat agreed to relocate guerilla units to countries in the Middle East.

In Tokyo, senior officials judged that they had two new problems on their hands. There was, of course, the task of rebuilding Lebanon. Then, too, there was the matter of Israel, which had so far refused to withdraw its troops. From the Foreign Ministry's viewpoint, both issues were clearly intertwined.

As one source explained:

> We have every intention of working with America to reconstruct Lebanon. The United States has placed great emphasis on this—perhaps too much . . . [for] we have yet to hear America accept the fact that Israel conducted an aggressive forward-advance. . . . In contrast, [the Japanese government] felt a forthright position was required, and so we immediately demanded that Israel's military leave Lebanon at once.[56]

Also troubling the Japanese was the subsequent U.S. call for the pullout of all foreign forces still in Lebanon. From the Japanese perspective, it was merely an extension of "this very tolerant attitude" toward Israel. The same source observed:

> Tokyo feels that you cannot deal with Israeli, Syrian and Palestinian troops on the same level. The Syrian military entered at the request of the Lebanese government for peace-keeping purposes. Certainly, they later abandoned that pretext and did much that was unforgiveable. But there was at least a legal basis for their presence. . . . [Even] in the case of the PLO, there was [at least] an agreement in 1969 permitting a certain number [of guerilla units]. As for Israel, though, there was no legal basis at all. It simply carried out an invasion. [The United States] is thus gravely mistaken to demand a total military pullback while treating all combatants alike.[57]

Soon after, President Reagan retreated somewhat from this position. On September 21, the American leader, reacting to the slaughter of Palestinian refugees under Israeli control, called on Israel to withdraw from Beirut. Moreover, he announced plans to return U.S. marines to Beirut as part of a trinational peace-keeping operation. Yet the president again refrained from condemning Israeli aggression, as he restated the case for his earlier peace proposal that omitted the PLO.

To the Japanese, this new tragedy had still failed to correct the misdirection in U.S. foreign policy. More worrisome, though, it seemed to have darker implications for the PLO. In late 1981, ministry planners concluded that the radical minority of the PLO had allied itself with Syria to block Arafat's support of the Fahd plan. In late 1982, they judged that the veto power had grown. According to their assessment, the chairman might have emerged politically stronger from his success in negotiating the PLO pullout. Nevertheless, he would be more vulnerable internally if he should advocate peace with a country that had ousted the organization from Lebanon, had propped up a puppet regime in Beirut, and had been held internationally responsible for the massacre of innocent civilians. In Tokyo, it thus appeared that two sides that desperately needed each other were moving farther and farther apart.

In retrospect, Japan's policies toward the Palestine Liberation Organization arose in response to a broader array of concerns over the Persian Gulf region itself. Proceeding cautiously, Tokyo officials tried to steer an even course between existing relations with Israel and the United States and more recent demands for equity from the Arab world. Individually, the decisions behind the United Nations vote in 1974, the PLO office offer in 1975, Arafat's visit in 1981, and the criticism of Israel in 1982 differed in both nuance and substance. Collectively, however, they defined a diplomacy of symbols calling for greater balance on the issue of peace in the Middle East.

Notes

1. Personal interview with Takeo Miki, former prime minister of Japan, July 29, 1981.

2. Personal interview with Fumihiko Togo, former Japanese ambassador to the United States, July 21, 1981.

3. "Paresuchina Ketsugian, Nihon Kiken," *Asahi Shimbun,* November 11, 1974, p. 1.

4. Personal interview with a high-ranking Japanese official (hereafter cited as Source A), August 1982.

5. "Jimusho Kaisetsu Nara, Kento," *Asahi Shimbun,* February 5, 1975, p. 1.

6. Interview with Miki.

7. Ibid.

8. Ibid.

9. Interview with Source A.

10. Ibid.

11. Interview with Miki.

12. Personal interview with Koichi Tsutsumi, former deputy director of the Middle East and Southwest Asia Bureau, Ministry of Foreign Affairs, July 17, 1981.

13. Personal interview with Fathi Abdul Hamid, PLO representative in Tokyo, July 14, 1981.

14. Ibid.

15. "PLO Gicho, Honsha Kisha To Kaiken," *Asahi Shimbun*, July 15, 1975, page 1.

16. "Miyazawa-Foto, Gaiso to Kaidan," *Asahi Shimbun*, August 16, 1975, p. 1.

17. Interview with Tsutsumi.

18. Interview with Source A.

19. Ibid.

20. Ibid.

21. Interview with Tsutsumi.

22. Interview with Source A.

23. "PLO Wa Boryoku To Muen," *Asahi Shimbun*, April 22, 1976, p. 2.

24. Personal interview with Iichiro Hatoyama, former foreign minister of Japan, July 22, 1981.

25. Interview with Tsutsumi.

26. Personal interview with Toshio Kimura, president of the Japan-Palestine Friendship Commission, July 28, 1981.

27. Ibid.

28. Comments by several Palestinian National Council officials appear in "Iran-Iraku Senso Wa Dageki," *Asahi Shimbun*, November 19, 1980, p. 1. See also "Gulf Arabs Place Reins on Iraq," *Washington Post*, December 21, 1980, p. 23.

29. Interview with Hamid.

30. Personal interview with a high-ranking Japanese official, June 1981.

31. Interview with Tsutsumi.

32. "Bansu-shi, Gaiso To Kaidan," *Asahi Shumbun*, October 6, 1980, p. 1.

33. Saburo Okita, *Economisuto Gaiso No 252 Nichi* (Tokyo: Toyo Kiezai Shimposha, 1980), p. 170.

34. Interview with Tsutsumi.

35. Ibid.

36. "Sadato Daitoryo—Ito Gaiso To Kaidan," *Asahi Shimbun,* December 18, p. 1.

37. Interview with Kimura.

38. Ibid.

39. Ibid.

40. Ibid.

41. Ibid.

42. Personal interview with a high-ranking Japanese official, July 1981.

43. See transcript, "15th PNC Session Held in Damascus," *Intra-Arab Affairs,* April 13, 1981.

44. Interview with Kimura.

45. Ibid.

46. Ibid.

47. Personal interview with a high-ranking Japanese official, June 1981.

48. Interview with Tsutsumi.

49. Ibid.

50. Interview with Source A.

51. Ibid.

52. Ibid.

53. Ibid.

54. Ibid.

55. Ibid.

56. Ibid.

57. Ibid.

3

The Hostage Crisis in Iran

I feel some contradiction about our policy toward Iran. On the one hand, we must maintain our strong ties to the United States. But on the other, we must protect Japan's interests in the Middle East. . . . It's difficult to do both. —Masuo Takashima, former Japanese vice-minister of foreign affairs[1]

The detention of Americans in Teheran in early November 1979 loosened the major underpinnings of Japanese foreign policy. In Tokyo's view, the hostage crisis severely strained relations with the United States by sparking sharp differences over strategic, economic, and energy policy. Although the Japanese presumed that the incident was a temporary phenomenon, they feared that Washington's response complicated the long-term tasks of securing oil supplies and blunting the Soviet advance in the Persian Gulf area. To defuse an explosive situation, Japanese leaders employed a series of approaches designed to strike a balance between their friendship with the United States and their Middle East interests.

In late November 1979, Foreign Ministry officials first honed their policies to protect economic arrangements negotiated with Iran. They believed that success hinged on the ability to avoid offending either Washington or Teheran over the hostage situation. At that time, the core of their concerns was the agreements reached by Iranian Prime Minister Mehdi Bazargan and senior officials in the Ministry of International Trade and Industry (MITI) before November 4.

On September 5, the Iranian government informed Tokyo of its interest in reviving a joint venture that had been started under the Shah. Japanese construction on the project—a plant to produce petrochemicals, had been suspended in March 1979 when turmoil following the Shah's departure caused Mitsui and other participants to withdraw workers and temporarily halt the venture.[2]

Official word from Teheran on the Iran-Japan Petrochemical Company (IJPC) triggered MITI's interest. In a business sense, completion of the IJPC was vital. It constituted Japan's largest private overseas investment, committing nearly $2 billion in Japanese capital. Although Mitsui was the largest backer, more than one hundred companies and twenty banks participated indirectly as shareholders and lenders. As

41

one official emphasized: "We could not let the IJPC go down the drain. Its construction was 85 percent completed, and the cost of failure would have been too great."[3]

Besides the fear of corporate loss, MITI had an energy incentive for resurrecting the project. In 1979, Japanese companies had been hit hard by sharp decreases in petroleum imports. The major oil companies that supplied 66 percent of Japan's petroleum needs in 1978 imposed broad reductions, cutting back 1979 shipments by one million barrels a day. Most seriously affected were Mitsubishi, Mitsui, Ito Chu, and nine other firms not affiliated with the majors. In MITI's view, a promise to complete the IJPC might be linked to demands for more oil from Iran. Increased imports of petroleum would alleviate not only the recent shortage but also a more historic concern over oil cutoff.

As one senior official emphasized:

> Our first oil shock was in 1940, not in 1973. At that time, America stopped shipments of heavy oil because of what we had done in Manchuria and Shanghai. The U.S. boycott turned around the Navy that had opposed war with America, and forced it to move for Indonesia. From that lesson, we learned that an oil cutoff may have unforeseen political consequences . . . and may mean the difference between life and death.[4]

Intertwined with this energy concern was a diplomatic incentive for restarting the IJPC. In MITI's view, Iran was a geopolitical flashpoint. More than 70 percent of Japan's total oil imports passed through the Strait of Hormuz to the south of Iran. The Japanese feared that a breakdown in relations might prod Iran to tie up tanker traffic. More troublesome, though, was the possibility of a Soviet presence in the Persian Gulf.

Sandwiched between the Soviet Union and the Persian Gulf, Iran was seen as a fragile stabilizer in the Middle East. Senior Japanese officials were convinced that "Russia [would] move for the Persian Gulf if it gains a foothold in Iran." In their view, a Soviet shutoff of petroleum suplies would prompt a Western military response. As Prime Minister Masayoshi Ohira remarked to one advisor: "If World War III occurs, it will surley start in the Middle East."[5] In September and October 1979, MITI officials believed that the IJPC might strengthen Iranian-Japanese friendship, thereby forestalling an energy challenge to Tokyo or a diplomatic tilt toward Moscow.

Armed with these concerns, the MITI vice-minister for international affairs, Naohiro Amaya, led a delegation to Iran on September 7. His purpose was to confirm Iranian interest in the IJPC. To the vice-minister's surprise, Prime Minister Bazargan attended the meeting. According to Amaya:

> [The Iranian leader] stressed the strong desire of the government to complete the IJPC as soon as possible. Bazargan said that he wanted the project to become a monument to the revolution and asked for help from the Japanese government. Direct assistance, he continued, would cause Iran to view Japan as a friendly country. . . . Of course, he did not say that a refusal would lead to unfriendly relations.[6]

But the implication was there.

During the discussion, Amaya pressed for an increase in oil shipments to Japan, and Bazargan apparently agreed. When the meeting ended, Amaya left with the impression of Iranian reasonableness and Teheran's strong desire to complete the IJPC. In his judgment, the Japanese government had no reason to delay the project any longer.

On October 13, Amaya returned to Iran with MITI Minister Masumi Esaki. At that time, Esaki informed Iranian Oil Minister Ali Akbar Moinfar of Japanese government plans to restart the IJPC. Esaki said that Japan would make the IJPC a national project, thus qualifying it for a $100 million subsidy from the Overseas Economic Development Fund, and $400 million in credits from the Import-Export Bank.[7] The next day, the MITI minister asked Bazargan for a 30 percent increase in oil shipments from Iran. Evidently satisfied with the IJPC proposal, Bazargan agreed to draw up term contracts raising Tokyo's oil allotment from 460,000 to 530,000 barrels a day. The contracts would be negotiated between the National Iran Oil Company (NIOC) and Japanese firms and would take effect from December 1979.[8]

Three weeks later, Tokyo's happiness with Iranian relations quickly changed. News concerning the detention of Americans in Teheran stunned the Japanese leaders. In their view, it was a reprehensible violation of human rights and international law. Despite private outrage, senior officials decided to respond quietly to events in Iran. They concluded that the stakes were too high for them to gamble. As one official quipped, "The IJPC was our hostage."

Another reason for restraint was the belief that the hostage situation would soon end. According to the deputy director of the Foreign Ministry Middle East Bureau, Koichi Tsutsumi: "We felt that the Americans would be released within two or three months. We never thought the situation would drag on."[9] Evidently, senior ministry officials judged that Japanese-Iranian normalization could resume after early release of the hostages. Meanwhile, Japan must sit tight and avoid blistering attacks that the Iranians would remember long after the Americans returned home.

As a consequence, the Foreign Ministry muted public criticism. Although France, Great Britain, and West Germany immediately condemned the Iranian action, Japan refrained from voicing official concern for a month. In early December, Japan's ambassador to the United Nations issued an ambiguous statement deploring the situation in Teheran.

Throughout November, senior ministry officials had also worried about Japanese actions that might offend Washington. Specifically, they feared attempts by Japanese companies to soak up petroleum pouring onto the spot market following the U.S. decision to boycott Iranian oil on November 12. Fumihiko Togo, the Japanese ambassador to Washington, realized that large Japanese purchases of Iranian oil at high spot-market prices would be viewed dimly by the White House.[10]

Top Foreign Ministry officials apparently reached the same conclusion. In late November, they asked the MITI minister to order Japanese companies not to buy spot-market oil. Although the minister agreed, Japanese firms purchased over half the petroleum formerly bound for America at a figure nearly double the posted Iranian price.[11]

There are two different versions of what happened. According to one senior official, lower-level MITI bureaucrats and Japanese companies ignored the minister's orders. As he recalled, "We were furious when we learned about the situation."[12]

A second official attributed the result to the mechanics of implementation:

> The problem involved the difficulty of overseeing twelve companies purchasing spot-market oil. We didn't know how much the companies had bought individually or collectively before the order not to purchase went out. Moreover, we had a time lag to contend with. Though the companies complied with our wishes to withdraw from the spot market, oil still flowed into Japan two weeks after the order to stop purchases. This oil came in on tankers that were en route to Japan when the decision not to buy was made.[13]

Regardless of the reason, the policy goal of escaping U.S. criticism soon evaporated. On December 10, U.S. Secretary of State Cyrus Vance met Japanese Foreign Minister Saburo Okita in Paris. The secretary's tone clearly surprised Okita. Vance tore into the foreign minister, criticizing Tokyo for insensitivity on the hostage issue. On a scale of one to fourteen, the secretary of state gave Japan a one rating for its concern about the Americans in Teheran. Then he chastised Okita for allowing Japanese firms to purchase large amounts of Iranian petroleum at inflated prices and charged that Japanese leaders had helped Iran circumvent the assets freeze imposed by the United States on November 14.

More disturbing for Okita was the public relations effect of Vance's attack. While Vance conferred with Okita, Parisian television reported that the American secretary was warning the foreign minister about Tokyo's policy toward Iran. After the meeting, Okita fumed about American insensitivity and Japanese humiliation resulting from the Vance episode. As one diplomat commented: "It's one thing to express U.S. displeasure privately, but quite another to do so publicly."

In Tokyo's view, American condemnation through the press was aimed at Western Europe as well as at Japan. Senior Japanese officials believed that Vance's earlier private requests for assistance from European Economic Community (EEC) leaders had been rebuffed. In their estimate, the secretary judged that a public raking of Japan over diplomatic coals might elicit the pledges of a common front that he had failed to secure.

Following the Paris meeting, Okita responded to the oil criticism with the promise to hold down Iranian imports to pre-November 4 levels. On the assets issue, however, other Japanese leaders responsible for banking policy were adamant. In their view, Vance's accusation was incorrect.

On December 17, U.S. Assistant Secretary of the Treasury Robert Carswell met Finance Vice-Minister Takehiro Sagami. The U.S. representative repeated Vance's claim of a Japanese end run around the assets freeze. Sagami flatly denied the charge and asked for proof of Japanese wrongdoing. Carswell declined, and Sagami bristled. The vice-minister then chided the assistant secretary: "Look, you are a lawyer. You ought to know that circumstantial evidence is not enough. You have to give us specific proof to support your allegations."[14]

In Sagami's view, Carswell's nonresponse stemmed from his wish to protect the U.S. banks that were leveling accusations against Japan. According to the vice-minister:

> We could easily find out which institutions had acted improperly, if the assistant secretary had only given us evidence. As you know, we have great control over our banks . . . for our laws are very strict. He probably refused to give us specific cases, because he would in effect reveal the sources charging Japanese irregularity.[15]

What particularly upset Sagami, though, was not Carswell's vagueness. The vice-minister felt that it was unfair for the United States to single out Japan for criticism. As he complained: "We all know that the German and especially the Swiss banks are up to funny business on the matter of an assets freeze evasion." Reflecting on U.S. intentions, however, he added that the White House probably thought it could use Japan to bring Western Europe into line.[16]

From mid-December, Japanese policy on the hostage issue entered
a new, more complex phase. Because of the Vance-Okita meeting and
to a lesser extent the Carswell-Sagami encounter, senior planners felt
that they had to contend with two uncertain actors, not one. As Okita
recalled:

> The hostage crisis was a very difficult problem for Japan. . . . A
> religious revolution had broken out in Iran. . . . In spite of that we
> had managed to keep normal ties to it. . . . About 12 percent of our
> oil came from that country; therefore, we didn't want to do anything
> that would damage relations with Teheran. . . . At the same time,
> there was the thinking that the Japan-U.S. relationship was the hub
> of our foreign policy. And that we would have to avoid any action
> that would harm it. . . . The domestic situation in America became
> quite emotional over the hostage issue, though. I therefore began to
> consider what policies would allow [us] to deal with Iran and yet not
> hurt our ties to the United States.[17]

During his plane ride home from Paris, Okita first told advisors
what he thought Japan should do. At some point, he said, the government would have to take joint action with the United States on the
hostage crisis. Several months later, the foreign minister refined the
definition of joint action to mean an alliance with the European Economic Community. Okita recalled:

> As one way of dealing with the situation, I looked to Western Europe,
> since its position was similar to Japan's. That is, its relationship with
> America was extremely important and it believed that the taking of
> hostages by Iran was a violation of international law. . . . Moreover,
> with the possible exception of Great Britain, the European countries
> were heavily dependent on the Persian Gulf region, on Iran for their
> oil supplies. For them [and for Japan], deteriorating relations with
> Iran would mean deteriorating relations with the Middle East itself.[18]

In Okita's view, a Japanese-European connection would serve several purposes. Most important, it might restrain the United States. The
foreign minister believed that among the major powers, the United
States had the greatest influence in the Middle East. Japan and the
West could enjoy stability there if Washington would work to "reduce
conflict and tension in the region." Conversely, they would suffer if
the United States should inadvertently push the region toward collapse.

Particularly disturbing to Okita and other senior planners were later
statements from Washington and meetings with U.S. officials that seemed
to underscore U.S. frustration over the situation in Iran. One source
related that U.S. leaders appeared to be "psychologically abnormal."[19]

Certainly, Japanese planners sympathized with Washington's diplomatic plight, but they also feared White House overreaction and the adoption of measures leading to Middle East instability and world war. Okita, Ohira, and other decision makers specifically worried that Washington might apply harsh economic sanctions or a naval blockade against Teheran. In their view, such steps would strangle Iran and fan internal chaos. Under those circumstances, the changes of Soviet ascendancy would improve. If Moscow did not enter to take advantage of Iranian disorder, the Soviets might be asked in by Marxist radicals, who the Japanese believed would rise from the political rubble.[20] According to one senior official: "We feared that Washington might give Iran to Moscow on a silver platter." To Okita and Ohira, joint Japanese and European support might lessen U.S. feelings of isolation and the possibility of an unwise policy charge.

Besides calming frayed American nerves, Japanese policy coordination with the EEC might help the United States in another way. Japanese leaders felt that the hostages must be freed. After January 1980, Ohira became exasperated with Teheran's behavior. Alternating signals of early release and quick denial exhausted the prime minister's patience. He reluctantly concluded that Iranian leaders could not be trusted. A common front with Western Europe, Ohira judged, might be the best approach under the circumstances. In the opinion of his senior advisors, economic sanctions alone would be ineffective. After all, they had failed in the case of South Africa. Moreover, the Soviet bloc could easily undermine the Iranian boycott by reselling Western goods to Teheran. A diplomtic merger with the EEC might be different, however. Although the measures themselves would have little consequence unanimous support by Japan and Western Europe might jolt Iranian leaders. Ministry officials believed that Allied solidarity could impress Teheran with the seriousness of the situation and force a reconsideration of hostage policy.

Several key decision makers also favored joint action for another reason. In their view, this would mark the first time that Japan and Europe had cooperated diplomatically on a purely political question with global implications. They felt that prior multilateral ventures with the EEC had been forged in the General Agreement on Tariffs and Trade (GATT) and in other economic forums.[21] On Iran policy, however, the EEC would finally accept Japan as a diplomatic equal. From the Japanese perspective, that precedent made their efforts worthwhile. In early 1980, these officials foresaw Japanese-EEC movement on measures guaranteeing Middle East peace. While uncertain whether a rival to the Camp David accords would emerge, they were hopeful that the basis had been laid for EEC cooperation on the Middle East and other difficult political problems.

Apart from this advantage, the Japanese believed that the EEC alliance would protect Tokyo from two forces: Teheran and Washington. The Foreign Ministry felt that Iran would be less likely to retaliate against Japan if Tokyo operated as part of a larger diplomatic unit. In hindsight, Vice-Minister Takashima judged that this policy succeeded.[22] Teheran did not dismantle the IJPC, despite threats to turn the project over to Yugoslavia. Equally important, Iranians did not harm the 1,000 Japanese living in Iran. As one official said, "Our people may be in Iran for their own profit. But they are still serving the national interest."[23]

Ministry officials also believed that a common front might protect them against unreasonable demands from Washington. On several occasions, Japanese leaders made the IJPC's exemption from economic sanctions a condition for support of an Allied boycott. Tokyo felt that the project must proceed despite new problems, including the unavailability of raw materials and the withdrawal of U.S. subcontractors, that clouded the IJPC's future. As one official commented: "Certainly, the economic loss resulting from IJPC failure would be great. But the political cost of abandoning the project now would be even greater."[24] Despite its reservations, Washington agreed. As a result, Mitsui's negotiations with Iran over the IJPC continued at a frenzied, nonstop pace.

The EEC tie would also permit Japan to deflect another U.S. demand. On April 8, U.S. Ambassador Mike Mansfield informed Vice-Minister Takashima of White House wishes regarding a diplomatic break with Iran. According to Mansfield, Washington might ask Japan to end official relations if sanctions failed to win the release of the U.S. hostages.[25] The Foreign Ministry responded with a polite but firm no. In its judgment, such action could crack Tokyo's fragile ties to Teheran and tip the delicate balance of energy and security interests against Japan. Tokyo offered one concession, however. As part of any boycott package, the ministry would recall the Japanese ambassador to Iran, along with similar moves by the EEC countries. Even then, however, Tokyo would disclaim any punitive purpose and would color the return in the neutral tones of a diplomatic consultation.

Coinciding with this internal shift toward multilateralism with Europe were more ominous calls for help from the United States. On December 21, 1979, the Carter administration had announced that it would ask the United Nations Security Council to institute economic countermeasures against Iran. Then, following a Soviet veto on January 13, Washington delayed unilateral implementation in hopes of an imminent breakthrough. When that did not occur, the U.S. president decided on April 7 to impose a general boycott and to break diplomatic relations with Iran. Furthermore, he elected to press the Allies more aggressively for collective economic sanctions. As a result, Secretary Vance met on the April 9 with the Washington representatives from Japan and twenty-four other countries to make the case for a nonfood boycott and withdrawal of the various ambassadors to Teheran. The next day, President Carter repeated this request for Allied assistance, while reserving the right to use military force against Iran.

Initially, Tokyo officials believed that they would have to do something. Okita and others judged that refusal would be a go-ahead signal for hasty decisions in Washington and unfortunate consequences throughout the Middle East. What transformed this judgment into movement with the EEC was a request for support from the Europeans themselves. As Okita recalled:

> The EEC countries asked for Japanese cooperation . . . [since] on both sides there was this sentiment for a common policy. From the European viewpoint, any economic measures taken without Japanese participation would be riddled with a big hole. This was the concern among the European countries. And they therefore had great interest in what Japan would do.[26]

The first formal indication of this interest in joint action with Japan came after the EEC foreign ministers' conference in Lisbon on April 10. According to press reports, the delegates were divided on the U.S. administration's policy toward Iran. The majority opposed collective economic sanctions, judging that some action would undermine their interests in Iran and would have little impact on the hostage crisis. In addition, the British, West German, and other ministers strongly opposed any reduction in their embassy staffs, believing that formal relations should continue undiminished. As a result, they adopted two measures that fell far short of White House demands. First, their ambassadors to Teheran would directly ask President Abolhassan Bani-Sadr for early release of the detained Americans. Second, the ambassadors would return to their capitals, ostensibly for debriefing.[27]

During those discussions, French Foreign Minister Jean-François Poncet raised another issue. In his opinion, Tokyo should be invited "to associate itself with the European initiative." His colleagues readily agreed, since, at that time, Japan's oil purchases accounted for over half of Iran's $4.2 billion in foreign exchange earnings.[28] It was apparently felt that Japan's support would give the EEC effort greater visibility in Washington as well as in Teheran.

On April 11, the Italian ambassador to Tokyo broached the European appeal to Okita and other senior Japanese planners. Acting swiftly, the Foreign Ministry first ordered its ambassador to Teheran to join his European counterparts in their meeting with Bani-Sadr on

April 12 and to return to Japan for consultations on April 16. Okita apparently believed that additional measures would have to wait until the next conference of EEC foreign ministers, set for April 21. Meanwhile, other Japanese officials responsible for economic policy made another decision that also appeared to back Washington against Teheran.

On April 18, MITI leaders announced that the government would refuse to purchase Iranian oil at the $35 figure demanded by the NIOC. Several days later, the Iranian Oil Ministry responded with a petroleum embargo against Japan. In the United States, news of MITI's decision was widely hailed as a sign of friendship. The real policy prop, however, was Japanese self-interest.

At first, MITI believed the price was unjustified. Coming only two months after a February increase, the $35 tag exceeded the common purchase price by $2.50. More worrisome, though, was the concern that acceptance might boost OPEC prices and harm Japan in the long run.[29]

MITI officials also felt that Japan could weather a shutoff. Tokyo had a 150-day stockpile on hand and could replace much of Iran's oil with increases from Kuwait, Qatar, and Mexico. MITI officials further assumed that Iran could not boycott Japan indefinitely. Senior Japanese planners doubted whether Eastern Europe or any other bloc of countries could absorb oil previously targeted for Japan. Moreover, they wondered how long Iran could afford to deny itself the $17 million that the Japanese oil business brought in daily. "Even the consumer nations," one official beamed, "have some bargaining chips."

Besides economic factors, political considerations weighed heavily in the decision to reject the price demand. MITI officials shared Foreign Ministry concern over American nervousness. The Vance-Okita scrap about Japanese oil purchases was still fresh in their memories, and they wished to avoid another bureaucratic brawl. A suspension of oil shipments from Iran thus seemed to be inevitable. As Vice-Minister Amaya explained: "We didn't want to do things that would excite America. . . . This was the basis of our response [to the $35 demand]."[30]

With this agreement against Iran's pricing policy in place, Okita left for Luxembourg on April 19 to discuss further action with the EEC foreign ministers. Before arriving there, he had more or less thought through what Tokyo should do. As far as the Japanese foreign minister was concerned, the dual objectives of helping America and safeguarding Iran could best be served by policies that fell somewhere in between.

First, any new diplomatic venture with the Europeans must avoid the appearance of permanent sanctions against Teheran. Of greatest concern to Okita was the need to sidestep an agreement compelling the Allies not to purchase oil from Iran. In his view, the recent decision by MITI was "purely economic"[31] A total boycott, he concluded, not only would mean irretrievably losing 11 to 12 percent of petroleum imports from Japan but also would needlessly shake the economic and political foundations of Teheran.

Fearing that such action would foreclose the possibility of eventual reconciliation with the West, Okita also decided that whatever measures were adopted should be applied gradually. At the start, Japan and the EEC countries must refrain from calling the measures "sanctions." Moreover, both sides should employ a step-by-step approach that would build pressure slowly for hostage release. Such a policy would presumably give a Teheran beset by political infighting the time needed to form a cohesive response.

At Luxembourg, Okita conferred with Lord Carrington and four other European representatives. Since Tokyo was not a member of the EEC, the Japanese foreign minister could participate only on an informal basis. Procedural considerations aside, however, he received a fair and open hearing of his views regarding the hostage crisis. To Okita's delight, moreover, the EEC delegates shared similar feelings on how to proceed.

For the Europeans as well, the hostage crisis represented a tug-of-war between their allegiance to the United States and their interests in the Middle East. Though highly critical of the Carter White House for what they perceived as inconsistency and faulty crisis planning, the European ministers concluded that the situation in Iran was spilling over into the Western alliance. The need to prevent a further decline in relations with Washington, as well as a U.S. resort to force, spurred the decision to take collective action. When things get tough, President Valéry Giscard d'Estaing emphasized, "we will have to stand by the Americans even if they are deadly wrong."[32]

What resulted on April 22 was a mix of omissions and measures reflecting a compromise between two extremes. The EEC members decided not to back an embargo on oil from Iran, even though many of their countries had already joined with Japan in rejecting the NIOC price demand. West Germany, the largest European importer of Iranian oil, was reportedly most anxious to avoid sanctions that could lead to a long-term cutoff of those supplies.[33]

In addition, the members uniformly disagreed with the United States on the matter of relations with Iran. Like Japan, they felt that their positions in Iran would be better preserved by formal communications, not by diplomatic break. The EEC ministers therefore declined Washington's request to end their ties to Teheran, choosing instead to reduce embassy staffs and freeze the visa applications of Iranian citizens.

Furthermore, the Europeans opposed the adoption of harsh economic sanctions. The delegates believed that extreme action not only would push Iran into the Soviet camp but also would undermine their own ventures in that country. Italy, for example, had $3 billion worth of projects in Iran and negligible Iranian deposits at home to compensate for those losses. The result was the decision to ban only new contracts on exports and services to Iran. Apparently to add bite to this and the other two measures, the ministers also agreed that their countries would withhold permission for military sales to Teheran. Moreover, they would consider additional steps should decisive movement toward a solution not surface by May 17, the date of their next EEC conference in Naples.[34]

Okita was obviously pleased with the Luxembourg meeting; in his view, it had responded to U.S. requests for help in a way that would not topple Japan's ties to Iran. Ohira agreed with the assessment. On April 24, his cabinet decided to reduce the size of the embassy staff in Teheran, to place visa controls on Iranians seeking entry into Japan, and to refrain from signing new export contracts with Iran. Moreover, the prime minister indicated that he would personally inform President Carter of these decisions and ask Washington to forgo any military move against Teheran.

One day later, however, senior Japanese planners saw these efforts come under fire. While attending a Diet session on the April 25, Okita received a confidential message from the Foreign Ministry. According to the note, U.S. forces had just staged an unsuccessful attempt to rescue the hostages in Teheran. The foreign minister was astonished.[35] In Tokyo, Okita, Ohira, and other officials had assumed that President Carter would take a broader approach, giving the sanctions a chance and then employing a naval blockade as a last resort.

In Washington, however, sentiment for waiting any longer had finally run out. On April 11, President Carter agreed with National Security Advisor Zbigniew Brzezinski, Defense Secretary Harold Brown, and other key advisors that a rescue attempt would have to be tried. For the president and the majority of his confidants, the mission apparently was less a matter of choice and more a conclusion made inevitable by two key assumptions:

Assumption One: Nothing More Could Be Done Diplomatically. In early April, the negotiations with Teheran had collapsed, and it was generally assumed that neither additional U.S. sanctions nor Allied support could revive them. Among the top policymakers, only Secretary Vance remained sanguine on continuing direct dialogue and external pressure. Indeed, President Carter himself had concluded by April 7 that his administration was no longer dealing with kidnappers who operated beyond Teheran's control but with a hostile Iranian government whose belligerent actions were coming close to obliging it to respond forcefully.[36]

Assumption Two: Something Else Had to Be Done Quickly. Public pressure and personal sentiment could not be ignored. Political opponents, it was felt, were using the hostage issue to score points against the president. The American people were thought to be pushing for a punitive military strike against Iran. Furthermore, administration policymaking was "certainly not helped by the daily invocations by well-known television commentators on the number of days our hostages had been incarcerated." Finally, President Carter, believing the "national honor [to be] at stake," feared that "excessive passivity" would damage America's international standing.[37]

Major Conclusion: Among Nondiplomatic Alternatives, a Rescue Mission Offered the Least Risk. The Soviet invasion of Afghanistan in December 1979 shaped the assessment of nondiplomatic options. The best response was judged to be the one that would least disrupt the Middle East. Not only was it important to minimize the chance of a Soviet-Iranian alliance, but it was also imperative to keep open the possibility of building an anti-Soviet coalition with Moslem elements in the region.[38] As a result, a quick surgical strike that would directly free the hostages was preferred over a prolonged naval blockade that might yield a Teheran-Moscow axis. Within the Carter White House, two contradictory elements—effectiveness and restraint—thus combined to form the definition of success.

In Tokyo, reaction to the failed mission was divided. Some senior planners personally favored it, believing that President Carter, confronted with Iranian intransigence and U.S. public pressure, had no choice. As Fumihiko Togo, then a senior advisor in the Foreign Ministry, explained:

> What Iran did was outrageous. You simply cannot seize embassy people and hold them hostage. I think that the resuce attempt would have been made earlier had weather conditions permitted it. Of course, the [Japanese] press raised quite a fuss over the U.S. [operation]. But they would not have been so critical had the mission succeeded.[39]

The overwhelming majority of senior officials disagreed, however. From their perspective, moral indignation did not provide sufficient justification for military action. Indeed, the question of Teheran's ethics notwithstanding, they believed that countervailing considerations regarding Middle East security should have tempered Washington's decision making. In personal interviews, many of them expressed deep disappointment and sharply criticized America's disregard for the aftershock of such action. Moreover, they wondered how the United States could criticize Soviet intervention in Afghanistan four months earlier when it had just made a military move against Iran. According to one source: "We may not know all the factors that went into the decision. But based on what we read in the press, we can't call it a rational act."

Okita shared one of these concerns. In the foreign minister's view, his policies in Lisbon and Luxembourg had been based on the assumption that they might restrain America. Clearly, the last thing Japan and the Europeans needed was a limited strike that might quickly escalate into a general conflict.

Fearing a disruption of oil supplies, the foreign minister waited on the afternoon of April 25 for further word on the rescue attempt. When it did not come, Okita left for a scheduled press conference, where he tried to downplay the significance of the U.S. raid. He emphasized that both the Japanese government and Europe had hoped for a peaceful resolution of the hostage crisis. Further, he said that Japan would continue to cooperate with the EEC in seeking a settlement of the situation. Then, referring to the operation as "an unfortunate incident," the foreign minister embellished Vance's statement underscoring the limited nature of the move with the interpretation that it was not military in design.[40]

Several hours later, Okita listened to President Carter's televison address, which explained the steps leading to his decision and stressed the humanitarian aspects of this limited action. After the Carter speech, the Foreign Ministry publicly expressed its understanding of the U.S. position in light of the 150-day detention of American citizens. Privately, though, Prime Minister Ohira said: "I am very, very surprised. I simply cannot see why the United States, which had controlled itself for so long, would so something like that."[41]

In addition to this bleak assessment of the Carter White House, Japanese leaders generally agreed that the rescue mission had two unintended victims: the U.S. secretary of state and the hostages themselves.

In Tokyo, Vance appeared to be a policy outcast who opposed the operation. When he resigned on April 28, senior Japanese officials worried about his replacement. Despite his December blast, Vance had been highly regarded in Japan. Tokyo leaders often referred to him as a reserved gentleman who understood Japanese thinking. Evidently they were worried that a less steady person might assume the diplomatic helm. The appointment of Senator Edmund S. Muskie eased their concern. Japanese officials felt that Muskie and Vance were similar, and they apparently hoped that the new secretary of state would have the bureaucratic clout to keep Iran policy on a more even keel.

As for the hostages, Tokyo leaders judged that the resuce attempt had complicted their return and lengthened their stay. The Japanese evidently assumed that the mission had drawn the Americans even deeper into Iran's political struggle by making them more visible symbols that rival groups were manipulating to maintain or gain power. Tokyo officials privately estimated that the hostages would be released once "they [had] served their purpose." Presumably, that would occur when some political force emerged with enough strength to stand alone.

Aside from these negative developments, the Japanese saw one positive spin-off of the rescue operation. In their view, the mission had acted as a safety valve, releasing public emotion. They judged that President Carter would be free from domestic pressure and could therefore wait for the internal Iranian changes that would send the Americans home.[42]

Meanwhile, the Japanese leaders would have to place the hostage issue on a policy back burner. From their perspective, they had no choice. First, new uncertainty in Iran appeared to bar an early settlement of the crisis. In late April, arrests and deaths resulted from attacks on leftist elements by Islamic militants. In mid-June, violence again erupted when some 100,000 demonstrators of the People's Mujahedeen, the largest Iranian left-wing opposition group, were fired on by revolutionary guards near the American embassy. Adding to this sense of anarchy was a growing division within the Iranian government itself.

Religious leaders of the Islamic Republican Party, already in control of the parliament, were trying to wrest further power from the secular-liberal leadership of President Bani-Sadr. Arguing that the prime minister should be chief executive, Ayatollah Behesti proposed to install in that post an individual who, among other things, would be "committed to dear Islam." Making matters more confusing were nagging questions about the health of Ayatollah Ruhollah Khomeini and the grim prospect of greater unrest without him. In light of the situation unfolding in Iran, Japanese officials concluded that diplomatic negotiations regarding the hostages were infeasible for Iran at that time.

For Tokyo decision makers, another factor reinforced the prospect of continuing paralysis on this issue—namely, a new mood of pessimism regarding the future of Allied cooperation. For the foreign minister and others, the U.S. rescue mission had effectively shredded their diplomacy with the EEC. As Okita wrote:

> Two months after the rescue attempt, I attended the summit meeting in Venice [for the Allied heads of state]. The hostage crisis did not become a major topic of discussion. One reason was the ironic twist of developments. Japan had decided to work with the EEC in calling for a peaceful resolution of the hostage situation and adopting economic measures against Iran. Our attention was fixed on whether these policies would help end the crisis and live up to America's expectations. What nullified all of this were the strong misgivings over Washington's resort to force.[43]

Since the Japan-EEC diplomacy had failed to persuade Teheran or to deter the United States, the only approach left was the pro forma implementation of the economic measures promised at Luxembourg. On May 23, the Japanese cabinet went through the motions of supporting the EEC's Naples decision to terminate export and service contracts signed with Iran after November 4. Other than this, joint action regarding the detained Americans appeared to be dead.

Finally preventing further activity on this issue was an internal development. On June 12, Prime Minister Ohira died. The country had to turn inward—not only to choose a successor but also to chart the future of the Liberal-Democratic Party itself.

The factor that would make domestic politics particularly messy was the timing of Ohira's death. Before succumbing to a heart attack, Prime Minister Ohira had seen his official position under attack. On May 16, the opposition Japanese Socialist Party made its traditional bid to enact a no-confidence resolution in the lower house of the Diet. To its surprise, the proposal passed. Other factors in the LDP, hoping to unseat the prime minister, broke ranks with the dominant Ohira-Tanaka alignment to ensure approval through abstention.

The prime minister soon retaliated. On May 19, he announced that lower house elections would be held on June 22, the same day as the scheduled upper house contest. In political terms, the move made sense. Because of the unusual nature of Japan's electoral system, the LDP might substantially increase its slim majority in the lower house, where the prime minister is officially selected.

For the purpose of a lower house election, the country is divided into 130 districts, each of which sends three to five members to that body. In the previous contest, in October 1979, the LDP had an unusually high number of *jiten,* or first-place finishers among losing candidates. A fourth-place vote-getter in a three-man district, for example, is a *jiten*. Of the 130 *jiten* in that election, the LDP had 54, or 41 percent of the total.

By calling for a lower house contest together with the upper house one, Ohira evidently intended to shrink the resources available to opposition-party Diet members who had placed last among the 1979 winners (for example, third in a three-man district) and were thus vulnerable to the challenges of LDP *jiten*. Presumably, a large victory by the LDP on June 22 would enhance Ohira's stature and quiet his LDP rivals.

News of Ohira's death came in the midst of preparations for this complex campaign. When the LDP strengthened its hold on the lower house from 258 seats to 284 seats, the members had to immerse themselves in the task of finding a party president who could keep the LDP together and, with its unanimous endorsement, be elected prime minister of Japan. The eventual winner was a dark-horse candidate, Zenko Suzuki.

As a Diet member whose diplomatic experience had been limited to oversight of the Japanese-Soviet fisheries negotiations in 1977, Suzuki was generally considered unqualified for the chief executive position. Political commentators, mimicking a slogan of the 1976 U.S. presidential election, often asked "Suzuki who?" To his credit, though, Suzuki had the political pull to keep the Ohira faction and its alliance with the Tanaka faction intact. Moreover, the new prime minister had the wisdom to place in his first cabinet two distinguished individuals, Kiichi Miyazawa and Masayoshi Ito, on whose advice he could depend.

Prime Minister Suzuki, Chief Cabinet Secretary Miyazawa, Foreign Minister Ito, and their advisors in the bureaucracy first decided that the fate of the U.S. hostages in Iran was beyond their control. Any initiatives to break the deadlock between the United States and Iran would have to be taken by one of the antagonists. Meanwhile, Japan should do what it could to strengthen its ties to Teheran. In July, Japanese workers returned to Iran to resume construction on the IJPC. Several months later, Tokyo tried to widen its channels of communication to Iran. The opportunity for this came unexpectedly from Iran.

On November 2, Teheran officially announced its four conditions of release for the detained Americans. The start of hard bargaining not only prompted Suzuki to express guarded optimism on an end to the crisis but also suggested that Tokyo could soon discard its self-imposed limits on relations with the Islamic republic. Because of the detention of the Americans, the Japanese government had to weigh all wishes for Iranian friendship against the alliance with Washington. The result was a plus-minus effect. Whatever Japan did to comply with U.S. requests constrained any effort to secure its interests in Iran. Certainly, Tokyo officials had kept the IJPC from becoming a victim of this calculus. Now, however, with the release of the Americans in sight, they might have greater leeway in finding other openings to the Middle Eastern capital.

In late January 1981, the Japanese made their first move. On January 23, two days after the American hostages were set free, the Suzuki cabinet formally decided to abolish the vestiges of the Luxembourg agreements. In addition to lifting visa restrictions against Iranian citizens and rebuilding their embassy staff in Teheran, Tokyo leaders officially ended the trade prohibitions in effect since April 22. From a business point of view, the decision clearly would help Iran. Monthly purchases of steel, textiles, chemicals, and other products had totaled $200 million, thus making Japan Iran's largest trading partner. Although the Iran-Iraq war threatened to disrupt the orderly flow of exports, Japanese companies appeared to be confident that new monthly sales could go as high as $150 million.[44]

Still, there was one item that senior officials considered to be far more important—oil. The prime minister, the Foreign Ministry, and MITI had wanted to abandon the oil boycott of April 1980. They believed that new arrangements on petroleum imports might help "keep relations alive" with an Iran that had been internationally isolated by the hostage crisis and unexpectedly buffeted by its conflict with Iraq. As one key decision maker explained:

> We would be happy if [oil agreements] permitted us to have strong relations with Iran. It will remain a very important element in the Middle East, not only as a supplier of oil, but [also] from a strategic point of view. So basically, we want to have friendly relations with that country. Right now, though, we don't know what sort of government they are going to have.[45]

While perceiving the long-term advantages of such arrangements, Japanese leaders also recognized an immediate impediment to them. The decision by Saudi Arabia, Jordan, and other Arab moderates to support Baghdad suggested that adverse reaction might result from petroleum deals with Teheran. For their part, senior Japanese officials were willing to counterbalance new purchases from Iran with new purchases from Iraq. After all, one source emphasized, it would not be in Tokyo's interest to buy the ill will of one or both countries. Even so, decision makers appeared to worry whether the Saudis and others would focus only on the agreements with Iran and incorrectly conclude that Japan had shed its neutrality toward the war.

Subsequent developments suggested that the Gulf States would not do so. In the weeks following the start of the conflict, Iranian oil production had slumped from 800,000 barrels a day to 100,000 barrels-a-day. In November and December, production gradually began to increase. By January 1981, it took a sharp upswing, with published estimates placing the new daily production figure between 750,000 and one million barrels. Throughout the first half of January, India, Spain, and the Soviet Union took advantage of this situation by signing new delivery agreements totaling some 290,000 barrels a day.

More significant, though, two major oil companies appeared to be on the verge of finalizing arrangements with the NIOC. On January 29, it was reported that Shell had just agreed to a 100,000-barrel-a-day contract at $37 a barrel and that British Petroleum (B.P.) was close to closing its own 75,000- to 80,000-barrel-a-day deal.[46] In Tokyo's view, the two majors apparently just passed a diplomatic acid test. Shell and B.P., clearly parts of the Allied establishment, had been able to buy Iranian oil without evoking moderate-Arab resentment. The way seemed to be clear, therefore, for similar moves by Japanese firms.

To assure that these purchases would stay within the parameters of acceptability to Iraq's backers, MITI and the prime minister's office did two things. First, they informed Japanese companies of the rules governing any individual agreements with the NIOC. As far as Tokyo was concerned, the contracts must follow the precedents set by Shell and B.P. Thus, presumably, the total amount and the purchase price would not conspicuously exceed 180,000 barrels a day or $37 a barrel. Second, the government encouraged businesses to conclude separate petroleum arrangements with Iraq. Accordingly, Japanese companies signed oil contracts with Iran on February 3 for 180,000 barrels a day at $37.60 a barrel and with Iraq on February 10 for 200,000 barrels a day at $38.50 a barrel.[47]

Although these agreements ended one segment of policymaking, the hostage crisis promised to live on as a legacy with long-term implications for Tokyo-Washington ties. From the Japanese perspective, events between November 1979 and January 1981 pinpointed the Japanese conflict with the United States over strategic insecurity, political instability, and energy resources in the Middle East. As a result, although Tokyo officials welcomed the freeing of the Americans, they also feared that the problems related to their release would remain diplomatic embers hot enough to reignite controversy and clashes with Washington in the future.

Notes

1. Personal interview with Masuo Takashima, former vice-minister of foreign affairs, July 1, 1980.

2. Personal interview with Naohiro Amaya, former vice-minister for international affairs, MITI, July 15, 1980.

3. Personal interview with Takehiro Sagami, former vice-minister for international affairs, Ministry of Finance, July 11, 1980.

4. Interview with Sagami.

5. Personal interview with a high-ranking Japanese official (hereafter cited as Source B), July 1980.

6. Interview with Amaya.

7. "Sekiyu 30-pasento Zoryo Ni Doryoku, Iran Shusho Esaki Tsusanso Ni Hyomei," *Nihon Keizai Shimbun,* October 15, 1979.

8. Interview with Amaya.

9. Personal interview with Koichi Tsutsumi, former deputy director of the Middle East and Southwest Asia Bureau, Ministry of Foreign Affairs, July 17, 1981.

10. Interview with Fumihiko Togo, former Japanese ambassador to the United States, June 25, 1980.

11. "Iran Genyu Taibei Kinyubun, Hanbun Ijo Nihon Ga Kau," *Asahi Shimbun,* December 12, 1979, p. 1.

12. Personal interview with a high-ranking Japanese official, June 1980.

13. Personal interview with a high-ranking Japanese official, July 1980.

14. Interview with Sagami.

15. Ibid.

16. Ibid.

17. Personal interview with Saburo Okita, former Minister of Foreign Affairs, July 29, 1981.

18. Ibid.

19. Personal Interview with a high-ranking Japanese official, July 1980.

20. Interview with Tsutsumi.

21. Ibid.

22. Interview with Takashima.

23. Interview with Tsutsumi.

24. Personal interview with a high-ranking Japanese official, June 1980.

25. "Zenmen Docho Wa Konnan, Shusho Gaisora Kyo Kyogi," *Asahi Shimbun,* April 10, 1980, p. 1.

26. Interview with Okita.

27. "West Europeans Decline to Impose Sanctions on Iran," *New York Times,* April 11, 1980, pp. 1, 5.

28. Ibid.

29. Interview with Amaya.

30. Ibid.

31. Interview with Okita.

32. "Allies Set to Impose Economic Sactions on Teheran May 17," *New York Times,* April 23, 1980, pp. 1, 9.

33. Ibid.

34. Ibid.

35. Saburo Okita, *Economisuto Gaiso No 252 Nichi* (Tokyo: Tokyo Keizui Shimposha, 1980), pp. 100–102.

36. Zbigniew Brzezinski, "The Failed Mission," *New York Times Magazine,* April 18, 1982, p. 31.

37. Ibid., p. 62.

38. Ibid., p. 28.

39. Interview with Togo.

40. Okita, *Economisuto Gaiso,* pp. 101–102.

41. Ibid.

42. Interview with Tsutsumi.

43. Okita, *Economisuto Gaiso,* pp. 103–104.

44. "Yushutsu Shodan Mo Kakki," *Asahi Shimbun,* February 2, 1981 p. 8.

45. Interview with Tsutsumi.

46. "Iran Genyu Yushutsu Saikai," *Asahi Shimbun,* January 29, 1981, p. 9.

47. "Iraku Genyu, Tainichi Yushutsu O Saikai," *Asahi Shimbum,* February 11, 1981, p. 9.

4 The Soviet Union and Afghanistan

The use of military force and acts of armed intervention must be decreased. . . . And so, we opposed the Vietnam invasion of Cambodia and the Soviet push into Afghanistan. —Saburo Okita, former minister of foreign affairs[1]

Soviet intervention in Afghanistan in late 1979 forced a new strategic problem on Tokyo leaders. On a basic level, Moscow's move appeared to checkmate a concept of deterrence long held by the Japanese.

Throughout the post–World War II period, senior Japanese officials had defined military security primarily in terms of Soviet threat and U.S. counterforce as they related to the Far East. In the late 1940s and early 1950s, Tokyo had looked first to U.S. conventional forces to stop a Soviet attack against the home islands. With the advent of massive retaliation, Tokyo subsequently relied on U.S. nuclear weapons for external protection.

At the same time, the Japanese developed their range of contacts with Communist China, Southeast Asia, and the Soviet Union slowly and sometimes sporadically. They did so, however, not from weakness but with a sense of relative confidence in their partnership with the United States and the security that it would provide. Broadly speaking, it was the U.S. tie that allowed them in the 1970s to normalize relations with the People's Republic of China (P.R.C.), support development of the Association of Southeast Asian Nations (ASEAN), and briefly consider a joint oil venture with the Soviet Union.

The new situation in Southwest Asia changed that, however. With Japan's primary interests expanded after 1973 to include the Middle East, the Soviet takeover of Kabul on December 27, 1979, threatened an area of the world where the U.S. shield did not extend. Senior Japanese officials, in the absence of a military option, would have to construct a diplomacy of deterrence to guard themselves against Soviet aggression. In Tokyo, consideration of policies and approaches emanated first from an analysis of Moscow's intentions.

Among core decision makers, assessments fell into two broad categories. One viewpoint, held by Foreign Minister Saburo Okita and others, focused on recent events in Afghanistan. Throughout 1979, domestic disorder had wracked two pro-Soviet regimes. Spreading insurgency by Moslem guerillas and an apparent coup by government ministers had led, in September, to the resignation of President Noor Mohammad Taraki. Despite continuing Soviet assistance, the administration of Hafizullah Amin appeared to be doing no better. Amin's rule not only had failed to curb the civil war but had led to factional divisions within political and military circles in Kabul.

Okita and other Japanese leaders placed this situation and the Soviet invasion in a larger historical perspective. According to the foreign minister:

> The Soviets are afraid of external invasion. They have the experience of Hitler and before that of Napoleon. They are thus very suspicious and I think oversensitive. . . . [In 1979] the domestic politics of Afghanistan became very unstable, and it appeared that the pro-Soviet [Amin] government was about to collapse. . . . This, they felt, would affect their security . . . and so they undertook a military invasion. The Soviets, I believe, adopted a policy of defensive expansionism, since they judged that the security of their own country was at stake. As for the effect, though, it was still an act of aggression.[2]

A contrasting, more dominant viewpoint was supported by Prime Minister Masayoshi Ohira and his other key advisors. This viewpoint also turned to history for guidance but looked on the darker side of Soviet intent. According to this assessment, the Communist leadership continued to dream the dreams of Czarist Russia for a warm-water port. They believed that it was the prospect of establishing year-round naval bases for operations in the Persian Gulf, Arabian Sea, and Indian Ocean—not the need for political housecleaning in Kabul—that prompted the Soviet drive southward.[3] Ohira and his advisors thus took a harsher view of Soviet action, believing it to be a blatant violation of territorial sovereignty.

Their differences of emphasis notwithstanding, the two groups of decision makers shared a common conclusion—that Moscow's military thrust could not be condoned, for it accented two larger, more foreboding trends of Soviet surge and U.S. slippage.

Soviet aggression in Afghanistan underscored a broad pattern of Soviet expansion throughout Asia. The massive buildup of conventional forces in the Northern Territories and the introduction of theater nuclear weapons near the Japan area had worried Foreign Ministry officials. Compounding this concern was the deterioration of Japanese-Soviet relations, reflected in the MIG incident and fisheries negotiations, and the revitalization of Soviet ties to Vietnam and possibly to India. Tokyo's anxiety over East Asia, however, was partially alleviated by Communist China. "As long as the Sino-Soviet rivalry continues," one official explained, "we seem to be relatively safe. But the Middle East is an entirely different matter."

In the ministry's assessment, the key to Middle East stability had been Iran, whose strength lay in its ties to the United States, not in its strategic firepower. From the ministry's perspective, it was the ability of the United States to use Iranian bases to undertake military action that had prevented Soviet penetration into the Persian Gulf area. In the opinion of one official, "Iran was safe even if it did nothing."[4]

Iranian security, this source continued, meant Saudi security. With a small population and a large land area, Saudi Arabia was vulnerable to attack. In the ministry's judgment, a stable Iran to the north had insured the defense of the largest oil producer. Kuwait, the United Arab Emirates, and other small countries were irrelevant in this security equation. The ministry assumed that these countries were too weak to resist an invasion and would therefore choose to ride out the course of events.

Despite this precarious situation, the Japanese thought that the Middle East was the region most ignored by the United States during the 1970s. For Japanese decision makers, the reason was an unfortunate lapse in U.S. military planning. According to one senior official:

> [The United States] allowed the Soviet Union to increase its military strength after the Nixon doctrine of 1969, and particularly after the Vietnam War. Can we call it the Vietnam syndrome? [The United States] allowed the Soviet Union . . . to take the lead, especially in [the field] of conventional forces. I'm sure that the West still retains a superior position in the [area of] nuclear deterrence . . . but it is not strong enough to keep the regional balance in the Middle East.[5]

As this source related, "this general lack of military thinking" led to a second oversight. He explained:

> I don't know whether [the United States] could have stopped the revolution in Iran. [But] I think the American government should have been able to put more attention on the situation there. . . . I wonder whether the people [in Washington] had sufficient realization of the possible disaster that revolution in Iran would bring.[6]

In Tokyo's view, these years of neglect held two implications for the Middle East. First, the United States had inadvertently contributed to Persian Gulf insecurity by putting all its strategic eggs in one basket. The Shah's departure, the Japanese believed, provided Moscow with an incentive to abandon its customary practice of military assistance in Angola and other third-world countries for a direct assault on Afghanistan. Such a move not only could be carried out with impunity but

would also better situate the Kremlin for entry into Iran and a drive
toward the Persian Gulf.[7]

Second, America would have to respond by playing a belated game
of conventional-force catch-up. Refusal to participate, Tokyo concluded, would leave the United States with two undesirable options:
sovietization of the Middle East or a massive nuclear counterstrike.

After December 1979, the Japanese followed with interest the new
U.S. effort to defense the Gulf area. Though giving high marks to the
rapid deployment force as a concept, they questioned whether it would
be deployable. Apart from Egypt and Oman, senior officials could not
conceive of any Arab country permitting a U.S. military presence on
its soil. Other measures—including base arrangements with Oman,
Kenya, and Somalia and plans for a permanent U.S. fleet in the Indian
Ocean—were viewed by the Japanese as distant solutions having no
impact on the immediate problem. As a result, Japanese decision makers believed that Tokyo and the Western Allies would have to do what
they could to ensure the stability of individual nations in the region.[8]
It was in this diplomatic mold that Ohira and his advisors cast Japan's
response to the situation in Afghanistan.

In their view, Tokyo's policy should pursue two interrelated goals.
Ohira and top foreign ministry officials believed that the Soviets would
have to pay for "adventurism" in Southwest Asia. At the same time,
Japanese leaders judged that the Kremlin must be deterred from taking
offensive strikes against Iran or Pakistan.[9] From their perspective, neither nation was prepared to defend itself from the 30,000 Soviet troops
and 200 Russian aircraft stationed to the north.

The Foreign Ministry felt that Iran was absorbed with its own internal difficulties, and—though it wanted to extend assistance—there
was nothing Tokyo could do. As one ministry official commented:

> At present, the [Japanese] government is unable to make any con-
> structive efforts [with Teheran]. They are so preoccupied with their
> own affairs. . . . And so we will have to wait until . . . they become
> more stable. Of course, I don't know [what] the future course of events
> in Iran [will be]—military coup d'etat or leftist takeover . . . just
> continuing confusion or consolidation of the present Islamic rule. It's
> difficult to say.[10]

The situation in Pakistan, though somewhat clearer, was hardly
encouraging. There was a government that, for the moment, appeared
to be better entrenched; but that regime, too, had had its problems.
Crop failure, soaring inflation, and mounting debt had strained Paki-

stan's resources. In addition, growing separatism among tribal and ethnic groups in the various provinces continued to challenge the rule of
President Mohammed Zia-ul-Haq. Adding further uncertainty were the
bloody clashes following Zia's refusal, in early April, to stay the exe-
cution of Zulfikar Ali Bhutto and Moslem attacks, in late November,
against U.S. cultural centers and U.S. citizens.

To stop Moscow's advance in this volatile region, Japanese leaders
decided to adopt measures conveying their disapproval of Kremlin actions. Despite a forceful tone, the specific policies amounted to political
jabs whose sting was more symbolic than substantive. In this sense,
they revealed the constraints and ambivalence of Japanese relations
with the Soviet Union.

While considering their response, Ohira and his advisors initially
recognized that they could not impose the wide-ranging, hard-hitting
bans and cutoffs of the United States. Tokyo's ties to Moscow were
less international than Soviet ties to America; therefore, the points
where Japan could apply pressure seemed to be fewer. Ohira and
Foreign Ministry officials also felt that the Japanese-Soviet relationship,
though strained, must not collapse. The possibility of oil exploration
in Soviet territory should not be foreclosed, and the resurgence in
bilateral trade must continue.[11]

Even more important, however, was the need to get along with the
Soviet Union itself. Since the Occupation period, the clear majority of
senior Japanese officials had neither liked nor trusted the USSR. The
Soviet seizure of the Kuril Islands, ill treatment of Japanese prisoners
of war, and other actions after World War II triggered strong anti-
Soviet resentment in Japan. Subsequent moves by Moscow, including
the broken pledges that nearly toppled the fisheries negotiations in
1977, did little to improve that image.

At the same time, though, Japanese leaders feared Soviet military
might and the USSR's geographic proximity to Japan. Particularly difficult to ignore in 1979 and 1980 were the seventy Soviet major surface
vessels and seventy-five antishipping submarines patrolling the Far East.
Referring generally to this buildup, Foreign Minister Okita reiterated:
"Good relations with the Soviets are important for us because they are
so close."[12] Senior planners, thus pulled by national need and limited
influence, felt compelled to contain their personal outrage. The result
was a mix of policies designed to reduce but not harm their relationship
with the USSR.

Apparently, Ohira and his advisors first agreed to avoid using the
term *sanctions*. The measures taken, in themselves, would of course

suggest that future aggression would entail future cost. Nevertheless, they must sidestep any characterization that might elicit the undying enmity of Kremlin leaders. "Japan," Okita said with a smile, "did not have economic sanctions. . . . [We] did express our displeasure though."[13]

The first mention of that displeasure was the Japanese announcement not to recognize the new Karmal government in Afghanistan and the decision to call in the Soviet ambassador for a "diplomatic discussion." On December 29, Deputy Foreign Minister Yasuei Katori met briefly with Dmitry Polyansky. During that session, the Japanese representative bluntly stated that Soviet forces constituted a grave threat to world peace and security. Tokyo, he continued, expected Moscow to stop its policy of interventionism and to respect the integrity and independence of Afghanistan. Polyansky replied by reiterating that his government was only complying with a request for assistance from the Afghan leadership itself. Furthermore, the troops would be withdrawn once the reason for their presence had disappeared.[14]

Katori remained unpersuaded, however. Noting that Afghan President Amin had been assassinated, he asked Polyansky who had extended the invitation? Evidently anticipating Polyansky's answer, the deputy minister argued that friendship treaties, such as those the Kremlin had signed with Afghanistan and other countries, could never make an unlawful act lawful.[15]

Nine days after the Katori-Polyansky meeting, other more specific parts of Tokyo's policy emerged. The broad framework appeared to be provided by the United States. In the prime minister's office, Ohira evidently decided to pattern Japan's response after the White House position; within the circle of concerns over Moscow, he wanted to do whatever was possible to reinforce Washington's actions. "Mr. Ohira," Okita wrote, "had been personally trained by [former] Prime Minister Shigeru Yoshida. As a politician and bureaucrat, he therefore clung to the conviction that cooperation with the United States was the centerpiece of Japan's foreign policy."[16]

On January 4, 1980, President Carter issued his official statement. Alluding to the "contagious disease" of aggression, the U.S. leader announced plans to block delivery of 17 million metric tons of grain ordered by the Soviet Union. Moreover, America would end the sale of high-technology items to the Soviets until further notice, curtail Soviet fishing privileges in U.S. waters, and delay scheduled openings of consular facilities in the United States and the Soviet Union. A continuation of aggression, he also warned, might jeopardize his country's participation in the Moscow Summer Olympics.

In Tokyo, senior officials tailored the Carter speech to fit their own diplomatic situation and policy objectives. On January 7, the prime minister unveiled a three-point program to buttress earlier support of a Security Council resolution demanding Russian withdrawal from Afghanistan. Besides reviewing the export of computers and other high-technology items, Ohira said the government would suspend official dealings with Moscow. Measures included a delay in talks scheduled between Diet and Supreme Soviet officials, a freeze on LDP meetings with the Soviet ambassador, and a refusal of the government to welcome future visits by the Soviet foreign minister.

As part of this package, Ohira also declared that Tokyo would temporarily shelve Siberian development projects that had recently been negotiated with Moscow. According to the prime minister, the Import-Export Bank would stop credits to three joint ventures—a forestry development, pulp manufacture, and harbor expansion agreement amounting to $1.2 billion.

Apart from the high-technology boycott, Tokyo's program seemed to lack a substantive bite. Although the government snubbed Soviet representatives, the basic diplomatic relationship remained intact. Also, although three new projects might have been scratched, older coal, petroleum, pulp, and natural gas ventures totaling $5 billion went untouched.[17]

Several weeks later, Ohira took another symbolic slap at the Soviets. On February 2, the prime minister announced that Japanese participation at the Summer Olympics would be inappropriate, given Moscow's continued presence in Afghanistan. Of the four measures, the Olympic boycott proved to be the most difficult. Whereas the three-point program involved measures that Tokyo could execute unilaterally, a boycott would require approval from an outside agency, the Japan Olympic Committee (JOC).

A tussle soon ensued between the JOC—headed by Katsuji Shibata, a former boxer—and three emissaries from Ohira—Foreign Minister Saburo Okita, Education Minister Senichi Tanigaki, and Chief Cabinet Secretary Masayoshi Ito. The JOC fought hard to go to Moscow, despite a weak position. Unlike its British counterpart, the JOC depended entirely on the government for financial support. All Olympic expenses were covered by national budget allocations to the Japan Sports Federation, of which the JOC was a member. Although theoretically independent, the JOC was in reality an umbrella organization with direct economic links to the government.

Following Ohira's call for a boycott, Okita, Tanigaki, and Ito met with Shibata on several occasions to convey the prime minister's wishes.

As the JOC chairman remarked: "Okita [and the others] didn't give me a hard time personally. . . . They simply said we couldn't have the quarter-million dollars for a trip to Moscow."[18]

Shibata and the JOC refused to yield immediately, however. They first decided to postpone an official vote on the boycott until May 24, the deadline for national organizations to file letters of intent regarding participation with the International Olympic Committee. Shibata and others held off on a vote in order to guage worldwide support for the Summer Games. As Shibata recalled:

> I was worried over the prospect of West Germany and all Asian countries deciding to go [to Moscow]. If it appeared that the only holdouts would be Japan and the United States, then Japanese athletes should of course be permitted to participate.[19]

While waiting for the international response, Shibata and the JOC constructed two proposals to circumvent Ohira's official preference. On April 16, Shibata floated the idea of allowing Japanese atheletes to attend as individuals, not as national performers. In his view, this approach had several advantages. It would permit participation in a manner consistent with Ohira's wish not to send a formal Japanese team. Moreover, the proposal would sidestep the question of government subsidy. Athletes who participated as individuals would pay their own expenses. Because this self-support stipulation would reduce the number of performers from 240 to 50, Shibata evidently felt that the unofficial team would be less conspicuous and therefore more acceptable to the government.

The disadvantage of this approach was obvious. It required a yes from Lord Killanin and the International Olympic Committee. When they said no, Shibata offered another solution. Under this formula, Japanese atheletes favored to win Olympic gold, silver, or bronze medals would be sent to Moscow. Though paying their own way, the individuals would participate as members of an official Japanese team. Shibata believed that the public would support a squad composed exclusively of judoists, women's volleyball players, and other world-class Japanese athletes. He apparently judged that such support might be used to pressure Tokyo into backing a smaller, financially independent national team.

Implicit in both proposals was the belief that Ohira could be turned around on the boycott issue. In Shibata's opinion, the prime minister's no-show policy became irreversible only after Ohira met with the U.S., West German, and Canadian heads of state in early May. Shibata believed that the prime minister painted himself into a corner at those meetings with promises to keep Japan's Olympic team home.[20]

After returning from his trip abroad, Ohira informed Shibata that Japan could not participate under any circumstances. To punctuate that point, the prime minister apparently threatened to withhold $7 million earmarked for the Japan Sports Federation the following year. As a consequence, Shibata urged JOC members to back government policy. After several heated sessions, the JOC formally decided on May 24 to boycott the Summer Games.

While settling their differences with the JOC, Japanese leaders put together a new set of policies based on a new set of assessments. In Tokyo, senior officials were generally delighted with the worldwide reaction to Soviet aggression. The developing countries, reportedly dismayed by the Soviet intervention in Afghanistan, had helped pass a U.N. General Assembly resolution deploring Moscow's actions. Within the Western camp, too, pressure was building. Canada and Australia had immediately joined Washington in canceling grain agreements recently signed with the Soviets. In addition, the EEC countries, though sharing Tokyo's concern about provoking the Soviets, had individually assailed the Kremlin for resorting to force and had collectively supported the British proposal calling for neutralization of Afghanistan and a Soviet military pullout.

Japanese planners believed that the measures, despite their unevenness, had at least sent the Kremlin two messages. First, armed intervention had meant a diplomatic setback for the aggressor state. Second, repetition of such "irresponsible behavior" would further deplete Soviet influence and goodwill around the world. The net effect, senior Japanese officials judged, had been to deny de jure recognition of an illegal act and, equally important, to reemphasize the premise that militarism would not go unchallenged.[21]

On a more pragmatic level, however, Japanese planners also realized that legal standards alone would not stabilize the situation in Southwest Asia. From their perspective, Soviet forces would never leave Afghanistan. After all, why should they? The Japanese believed that the Kremlin had certainly encountered heavier-than-expected resistance following its decision to invade Kabul. Not only had the diplomatic criticism been harsher than anticipated, but the 3,000 to 5,000 casualties suffered during the first two months of fighting had been higher than originally calculated. Nevertheless, the Japanese Foreign Ministry regarded these costs as minor nuisances rather than major challenges to Soviet dominance in Afghanistan. As one official explained:

Short-term, long-term . . . [Soviet forces] will continue to be in Afghanistan . . . in spite of the fact that we put pressure [on them] and in spite of the EEC proposal for an international conference, which

Lord Carrington discussed with Mr. Gromyko on July 6 . . . and despite this very strong opposition by many antigovernment elements in Afghanistan itself.

I think the Soviet Union is powerful enough to remain in the major cities in Afghanistan . . . [to keep open] its major routes of communication and [protect] the air space . . . powerful enough to keep them under control. That is all that is required to control Afghanistan.

Many people talk about the lack of Soviet control in the countryside, but the countryside is not very important. Historically speaking, no central government has ever had effective control over the entire country. What they did was just to have the capital and other major cities under government control.

The only difference is whether the government has the acquiescence or placid agreement of the people to be governed or whether [it is faced with] their overt opposition. Right now the Soviet Union and present regime in Afghanistan do not enjoy the popular acquiescence of the people. But in that case, military power is all that counts. And the Soviet Union is powerful enough to bear the cost of several million dollars a day for ten to twenty years. So short-term or long-term, there will be no change.[22]

Given the futility of trying to force the Soviets from Afghanistan, Japanese leaders concluded that the West should work to prevent the spread of a Soviet-dominated status quo farther south. For that, a new strategic balance would have to be erected. Ohira, Okita, and others firmly believed that power politics was the only way to deal with the Soviets. In their view, it was only through a position of strength that they could reach a common understanding with their nemesis.

Again, Foreign Ministry officials turned their attention to Iran and Pakistan. To them, Iran continued to be a sticking point in Tokyo's diplomacy. Because of the hostage crisis, they had to contend with the looming threat of U.S. intervention; and because of turmoil in Teheran, they remained unable to provide the help that might forestall Soviet entry. As a result, the ministry felt that Japan could do little else but work with Europe for release of the Americans, while hoping for consolidation of some anti-Communist regime in Iran and, ideally, for a reconciliation between Iran and the United States.

With regard to Pakistan, ministry planners had greater hope. The reason was the apparent upswing in Islamabad-Washington relations. Throughout 1979, the Carter White House had been at odds with the Zia regime. Pakistan, U.S. intelligence had charged, was acquiring the ability to produce nuclear weapons. Dissatisfied with Zia's denials, in early April the Carter administration had suspended the $80 million of economic and military aid earmarked for Pakistan. Nine months later, however, the president suddenly reversed that decision. With the military map of Southwest Asia redrawn by the Soviets, Carter said on January 4, 1980, that he would soon ask the Congress to restart direct assistance.

The Japanese Foreign Ministry was clearly pleased by the U.S. initiative, since, in its estimate, the $400 million package might keep Pakistan nonaligned as well as implicitly telling the Kremlin to stay out. On January 22, the ministry and Ohira indicated their agreement with the U.S. effort by extending $4.5 million to Pakistan for the half-million Afghan refugees who were exhausting Islamabad's resources.[23] Soon, Tokyo did even more.

During the next three months, Japanese leaders stepped up their assistance to third-world countries that provided a buffer between the Soviet Union and their Persian Gulf interests. Although the programs assumed the guises of economic development and humanitarian relief, they were, at heart, attempts to harden these strategic zones against Communist penetration.

Ohira and the Foreign Ministry made a new financial commitment to Pakistan. On January 25, Tokyo announced plans to offer Pakistan a $145 million package. That amount, a 230 percent increase over the 1979 figure, would be divided on a three-to-one ratio between low-interest loan and concessionary aid.[24] The government did not stop there, however. On March 4, Tokyo decided to send Islamabad an additional $1.6 million for the burgeoning Afghan population and to help it indirectly from the $4.5 million in new money donated to the United Nations High Commission on Refugees. One month later, senior officials also provided a nearby country, Turkey, with $100 million in emergency assistance. Then they turned their attention to Southeast Asia.

Japanese decision makers concluded that public displeasure over Hanoi's thrust into Cambodia would symbolically lift their commitment to Southeast Asia. The linkage was made on April 1 by the decision to follow a cutoff of 1980 aid to Afghanistan with identical action against Vietnam.[25] It was then strengthened on April 18 by a $2 million pledge to Thailand, another country forced to care for the refugees of Communist aggression.[26]

In addition to these grants-in-aid, the Japanese prime minister decided to do something else. On January 18, Ohira said that he would send a special emissary to the Middle East and Southwest Asia. His choice, Diet Lower House member Sunao Sonoda, was a former foreign minister with strong contacts in the Arab and Asian world.

Although the Foreign Ministry backed the general idea of bolstering both regions diplomatically, it strongly opposed two specific objectives that Ohira grafted onto the trip. The prime minister, to the ministry's dismay, agreed with Chief Cabinet Secretary Masayoshi Ito on the need for a stopover in Teheran. Ohira and Ito felt that meetings with President Bani-Sadr and others might create openings to a country made more vulnerable by Soviet aggression. Indeed, Ito implied, these discussions might even facilitate an early end to the hostage crisis.

Foreign Ministry officials remained unpersuaded, however. To them, a visit to Teheran was impractical as well as imprudent. Iran, they calculated, would be completely involved with the general election set for mid-March. Moreover, Japanese contact in the midst of efforts by the White House and the UN Secretary General to win release of the detained Americans might be seen as mindless meddling in a complex crisis.[27] Despite these arguments, the ministry lost for the moment. On February 4, the prime minister said that Sonoda would discuss economic cooperation and recent international changes with leaders in Teheran.

The next Ohira objective drew an equally cool response from the Foreign Ministry. As head of the government, Ohira wished to address the nagging problem of Middle East peace and therefore proposed to have his emissary meet Yassir Arafat in Damascus on March 1. From the ministry's perspective, the move made little sense. In its view, Japan was still unable to offer the diplomatic recognition that the PLO wanted. Moreover, high-level talks with Arafat so soon after the memorable Vance-Okita meeting would be enough to incite the United States again.[28] The prime minister overruled the ministry a second time, however, apparently in the belief that the potential benefits would outweigh the recognizable cost.

These areas of disagreement aside, the ministry enthusiastically endorsed the other two goals of the Sonoda mission. Tokyo officials, still shaken by the 1979 cutbacks of the major oil companies, wanted to lobby the producers themselves for stable supplies. Evidently using Miki's 1973 trip as their model, Ohira and the Foreign Ministry agreed to have Sonoda explain Japan's energy needs in the context of technical cooperation with the Persian Gulf States and support for Palestinian rights. As for Southwest Asia, they decided that the emissary would inform leaders of Tokyo's concern about Soviet aggression, along with its interest in closer economic relations.

On February 18, Sonoda departed for his four-week, seven-nation tour. To the ministry's quiet relief, the mission turned out quite different from what Ohira had envisaged. In Iran, Bani-Sadr had his hands full. The campaign for the parliamentary contest was starting up, and a United Nations commission arrived, in late February, to hear Teheran's side of the hostage crisis. Because of this situation, the Iranian president informed Tokyo that discussions with Sonoda were inconvenient.[29]

Occurring at the same time was another development that would also reshape the Japanese mission. In early February, informal talks started in Abu Dhabi between Ambassador Muratra and Arafat's representative regarding a diplomatic trip to Japan by the PLO chairman. This breakthrough and the availability of Toshio Kimura meant that Ohira could have it both ways. He could strengthen Japan's links to the PLO and yet spare himself the diplomatic grief arising from official contact. As a result, the decision was made to replace the Sonoda meeting with a nongovernmental approach by the Japan-Palestine Friendship Commission.

With the Iran stopover and the Arafat discussion thus omitted, the Sonoda tour became what the ministry initially thought it should be— namely, a more focused treatment of two more immediate energy and strategic problems. The discussions in fact allowed Sonoda to make some headway on both items, but they also reminded Tokyo just how intricate the situations in the two regions were and just what role Japan was expected to play.

In the United Arab Emirates, the first stop on his visit, Sonoda reviewed Japan's energy needs and Palestinian position with Oil Minister Mani Said al-Otaiba. As a strong advocate of Tokyo-PLO relations, Otaiba was anxious to confirm Japan's interest in a PLO initiative. What Sonoda said clearly pleased him. According to the special emissary, an invitation for an Arafat visit to Japan would be forthcoming from Toshio Kimura's group, the Japan-Palestine Friendship Commission. While in Tokyo, Sonoda added, the PLO chairman would naturally have the opportunity to meet Prime Minister Ohira and Foreign Minister Okita.

After hearing these assurances, Otaiba spoke of the importance his government placed on Japan. Soviet intervention in Afghanistan, he said, accented the broader threat of growing superpower competition throughout the region. The U.A.E. must therefore turn to Japan, Western Europe, and the United States for assistance in preserving its national independence. Otaiba then ended the meeting with a pledge to help stabilize the oil situation for Japan.[30]

Following talks with other U.A.E. leaders, Sonoda traveled to Iraq on February 24 for discussions with President Saddam Hussein and Deputy Prime Minister Tareq Aziz. There, the ideological orientation was different, yet the message was the same. While sidestepping criticism of Moscow, both Iraqi officials harshly rebuked the United States for trying to establish military bases nearby. That, they implied, would transform the Middle East into a battleground between East and West. To protect itself, Iraq would need support from Europe and Japan. To assist Japan, it would extend current oil-delivery agreements providing a 40 percent increase over previous contracts.[31]

In Oman, the next stop, Sonoda met with a pro-American leadership that was trying hard not to appear that way. Sultan Qabus bin Said had supported the Camp David accords and had discussed the establishment of military bases with the Carter administration. In his meeting with Sonoda, however, he couched his diplomacy in terms of assistance from the West and said that his talks with Washington were about facilities, not military areas. Semantics aside, Qabus bin Said asked Sonoda whether Japan might give a security guarantee for the Strait of Hormuz. When informed that this was out of the question, he replied that expertise in agricultural development and other such projects would be an acceptable substitute.[32]

On February 28, the Sonoda mission again dealt with the left. In Damascus, Syrian Prime Minister Adbul Rauf al-Kasm complained about the deficits that trade with Japan had caused. In his view, Tokyo must do two things: rectify the imbalance by offering yen-denominated loans and reinforce the economy by granting at least $100 million for power generators and other hardware. Evidently surprised by these requests, Sonoda agreed to study the loan proposal and to have the individual projects considered by a committee of experts.[33]

Two days later, Sonoda went to Saudi Arabia, where he first met with Prince Fahd. The Arab leader clearly judged Japan to be a potential impetus to the peace process. In scoring the Camp David accords, he equated Soviet action in Afghanistan with Israel's occupation of Arab lands. On March 2, 3, and 4, Saudi Oil Minister Yamani and other officials went a step further, implicitly linking help on the Palestinian issue and industrial development to stable oil prices as well as supplies.[34]

With the Middle East leg of his trip completed on March 6, Sonoda went to Southwest Asia, where he absorbed another round of complaints. In Islamabad, President Zia and his subordinates praised Japan as the first country to send aid and then derided Washington for not doing enough. In New Delhi, Prime Minister Indira Gandhi and External Affairs Minister P.V. Narashimha Rao welcomed Sonoda's offers of technical help and diplomatic support while condemning American arms to Pakistan, their adversary to the west.

Soon after Sonoda's return to Tokyo on March 13, Tokyo officials brought the policymaking phase of Afghanistan to an end. Some thirteen months later, however, they saw their diplomacy of deterrence under attack from an unexpected direction.

On April 24, 1981, President Ronald Reagan lifted the grain embargo against the Soviet Union. Among Japanese leaders, reaction ranged from angry comments to stonefaced silence. The more livid group of decision makers felt personally betrayed. Believing in the importance of solidarity with the United States, they had maintained their trade restrictions on Moscow even though others had not. Certainly Argentina's fourfold surge in grain, meat, and other exports to the Soviet Union came as no surpirse. What stung, however, were the attempts by several EEC members to take advantage of the slowdown in Japanese-Soviet trade. Evidently most painful was the French business takeover of a project that had been suspended by the high-technology embargo. Backed with credits from Paris, the Creusot Loire Group moved to fill a $350 million steel plant order that Moscow had awarded jointly to Nippon Steel and the Armco Steel Corporation of the United States.[35] To these Japanese leaders, the Reagan decision was particularly embarrassing because it showed the public and the business community what fools they had been.

The other group of policymakers phrased their disappointment in slightly differnt terms. The grain embargo, they conceded, had done little to hurt Moscow. Nevertheless, its importance lay in Washington's willingness to stand firm against the Soviets. In Tokyo, part of this resolve appeared to be the larger budget deficits that the United States would have sustain. When the agricultural ban was imposed, senior Japanese planners estimated that a system of purchase guarantees would be needed to prevent a sudden dumping of export grain onto the U.S. market.[36]

This steady drain on U.S. finances, and the election of a presidential candidate who opposed the embargo, obviously meant that the embargo would not last for a long time. Even so, the Reagan announcement was completely unexpected, for it came only three months after the president took office, and at a time when the possibility of Soviet incursion into Poland seemed to be growing. As one Japanese official explained:

> We feel that we have been faithful in observing our measures against the Soviet Union. . . . The important thing is to show them that this sort of armed intervention cannot be made without cost. . . . So frankly speaking, the lifting [of the grain embargo] was not very welcomed because it revealed a lack of consistency in [U.S.] action.[37]

Still more troublesome were other developments that threatened the very basis of Japan's diplomatic effort. In a fundamental sense, Tokyo's responses to Soviet aggression in Afghanistan revolved around the key premise of Allied cooperation. Although senior officials had formulated policies unilaterally, they realized that the effectiveness of these policies would depend on the degree to which they meshed with actions of the United States and Western Europe. It was for this reason that Okita said: "We have entered a new, more dangerous age. . . .

But by working together, Japan, America and Europe can have greater world peace."

A series of mishaps, however, and what the Japanese perceived as U.S. insensitivity, caused Tokyo-Washington relations to wobble badly. Ronald Reagan began his presidency, wanting the United States' two most powerful partners, West Germany and Japan, to assume a greater share of defense costs and responsibilities. In late March 1981, Defense Secretary Caspar Weinberger met separately with officials of the two countries to convey these wishes. Both the Japanese and the West Germans were noncommittal.

German Defense Minister Hans Apel avoided a specific pledge as he contrasted past German increases in military spending to U.S. decreases and denied reports that future expenditures would decline. Japanese Foreign Minister Masayoshi Ito was more vague, stating that his government could not participate in any collective security arrangement and would independently determine its own military budget within existing financial and constitutional constraints.[38]

One reason for Ito's reply was Tokyo's surprise at the suddenness of Reagan's defense demands. "Japan," one source emphasized, "is quite willing to do whatever it can. But the request [from Washington] came so soon." Another reason appeared to be a more deeply rooted concern with the military issue itself. In Japan, security policy arouses something more than just a pacifist versus realist debate. For both the left and the right, it has symbolized the extent to which the nation would continue to accept Liberal-Democratic Party rule and its pro-American orientation in foreign affairs.

In the 1950s, violent street protests against U.S. bases and the U.S.-Japan Security Treaty not only traumatized the nation but also expressed hardcore doubts about who should govern and how Japan could best protect itself. By the late 1970s, this polarization faded against a backdrop of unexpected international and domestic changes. New economic uncertainties linked to the oil shock, and a sense of strategic vulnerability against the Soviet Union, appeared to conservatize the electorate and reorder its agenda. Nevertheless, prime ministers and other politicians still treaded cautiously in the military sphere, regarding it as a powder keg that could easily explode.

To the consternation of Tokyo leaders in April 1981, the Reagan administration appeared to be bent on lighting that powder keg. In a follow-up speech on April 28, Secretary Weinberger pointed to the six-to-one disparity in military spending between Japan and the United States and called for a greater defense effort by Japan in the Northern Pacific. Feeling publicly forced to respond, the Foreign Ministry began to consider what position would avoid an antigovernment, anti-American blowup at home and yet satisfy Washington's demand for a more visible strategic posture. The ministry would have to work quickly, since Prime Minister Zenko Suzuki was scheduled to depart in early May for talks with President Reagan.

Within the Foreign Ministry, policy planning focused primarily on the joint communique. That document, normally released after heads of state had met, customarily framed the understandings on the issues most basic to any relationship. Because of recent events, the joint statement in Washington presumably would have to emphasize defense.

In the ministry's view, the communique should first stress the non-military half of Japan's security policy. This would be done through references to Tokyo's economic and political contributions to stability in Asia, its medium-range plan for development assistance to third-world countries, and its support for arms control between the super-powers. Other diplomatic elements, including statements on the need for comprehensive Middle East peace and controlled development of nuclear energy, also seeped into the final draft.[39]

Regarding military policy, the ministry tried to find a middle ground between what the United States wanted and what Japan could provide. The document would acknowledge the U.S. position regarding an appropriate division of roles in military affairs, and it would stipulate general pledges to increase defense capabilities and lessen the financial burden of U.S. forces in Japan. It would also, however, make all defense activities subject to the Japanese Constitution and omit specific steps that Tokyo would eventually take. The ministry felt that a U.S.-Japan security committee, scheduled to convene one month after the Suzuki visit, would be the appropriate forum for reviewing several delicate issues, including Tokyo's agreement to protect commercial sea lanes with a 1,000 nautical mile extension of Japanese naval operations.[40]

Finally, the ministry added an item that it considered both natural and innocuous. In the opening paragraph, the communique would refere to the "alliance" binding the United States and Japan. From the ministry's perspective, that term signified nothing new. Prime Minister Ohira had used it to describe the relationship with America. Then, too, there was the belief that the partnership, as defined by the U.S.-Japan Security Treaty, was based on an alliance concept.[41] In this sense, the term was the ministry's way of acknowledging diplomatic reality.

The completed draft was handed to Suzuki for review. He approved the document in its entirety, evidently trusting the judgment of individuals with greater expertise and believing that the communique reflected his own goal of soft-peddling the military issue while in Washington. Unfortunately, that did not happen.

When the joint statement was issued to the press on May 8, Japanese journalists ignored the passages on Tokyo's nonmilitary efforts toward regional peace and focused, instead, on the new military alliance that seemed to be evolving. Adding further confusion was a well-publicized round of contradictions by the prime minister and the Foreign Ministry. After returning to Tokyo, Suzuki denied that the term alliance implied a security relationship. Ito and other ranking officials, however, denied the denial, saying that Japan's alliance with America of course contained a military component. In their view, that was only common sense.[42]

Soon, political differences gave way to personal bitterness, with the prime minister questioning the ministry's competence and senior officials firing back that Suzuki had, after all, approved their draft. Judging that his position was untenable, Foreign Minister Ito took personal responsibility for the "alliance" flap and submitted his resignation on May 15. Nevertheless public rancor did not abate. Several days later, the Suzuki government was hit by another unexpected salvo.

In an interview with a correspondent from the *Mainichi Shumbun,* former U.S. Ambassador Edwin O. Reischauer confirmed the existence of an oral agreement permitting U.S. ships armed with nuclear weapons to enter Japanese waters. That understanding, arrived at twenty-one years earlier, violated one of Tokyo's three nonnuclear principles forbidding the introduction of such weapons into the Japan area. The press again attacked the government, despite denials by the new foreign minister, Sunao Sonoda. Japanese editorials openly doubted Suzuki's integrity as well as his ability to handle foreign affairs. During one news conference, a journalist bluntly asked the prime minister whether the nation was being run by a pack of liars.

In late May, Tokyo's defensiveness and public resentment against the United States dramatically surfaced in the decision to cancel the upcoming trip to Japan by Secretary of State Alexander Haig and in a demonstration by some 1,300 Japanese at the Yokosuka naval base. Far more unsettling, however, was the greater security dilemma represented by the domestic flareup of mid-1981.

After December 1979, senior Japanese planners had embraced a diplomacy of deterrence to protect Southwest Asia and the Middle East against Soviet aggression. Although the specific parts of that policy were formulated independently, they were implemented in the belief that Japan could not do it alone. Strategic success, it was judged, required the formation of a new consensus regarding the interests that the Allies shared and the contributions that each would make individually. In this respect, President Reagan's position on an arms buildup was most disappointing. It not only underestimated the ability of U.S. pressure to help galvanize antimilitary sentiment in Japan, but it also overlooked the need for close cooperation outside the Pacific region, where both nations were militarily weak and were threatened by a common foe. Overall, one official suggested, it ignored the fact that security is whatever makes you secure.

Notes

1. Personal interview with Saburo Okita, former minister of foreign affairs, July 29, 1981.
2. Ibid.
3. Personal interview with a high-ranking Japanese official (hereafter cited as Source B), July 1980.
4. Interview with Tsutsumi, former deputy director of the Middle East and Southwest Asia Bureau, Ministry of Foreign Affairs, July 17, 1981.
5. Ibid.
6. Ibid.
7. Personal interview with a high-ranking Japanese official, June 1981.
8. Interview with Tsutsumi.
9. Interview with Source B.
10. Interview with Tsutsumi.
11. Interview with Source B.
12. Interview with Okita.
13. Ibid.
14. Saburo Okita, *Economisuto Gaiso* No 252 Nichi (Tokyo: Toyo Kiezai Shimposha, 1980), pp. 30–32.
15. Ibid.
16. Ibid. p. 34.
17. "Gaimusho Hoshin: Afugan Kaiketsu Made Soren E Kansetsu Seisai," *Asahi Shimbun,* January 9, 1980, p. 1.
18. Personal interview with Katsuji Shibata, president of the Japan Olympic Committee, July 9, 1980.
19. Ibid.
20. Ibid.
21. Interveiw with Tsutsumi.
22. Personal interview with a high-ranking Japanese official, July 1981.
23. "Pakisutan No Afugan Nanmin 10-oku Enbun No Busshi," *Asahi Shimbun,* January 22, 1980, p. 1.
24. "Taipa Enjo 320-oku En Ni," *Asahi Shimbun,* February 26, 1980, p. 2.

25. "Taibetonamu, Afugan Enjo Toketsu," *Asahi Shimbun,* April 1, 1980, p. 2.

26. "Tai Ni 4-oku En," *Asahi Shimbun,* April 18, 1980, p. 2.

27. "Chuto E Sonoda Tokushi," *Asahi Shimbun,* June 29, 1980, p. 1.

28. "PLO To No Kaidan, Gaimusho Ga Hantai," *Asahi Shimbun,* February 22, 1980, p. 2.

29. "Iran Homon Chushi," *Asahi Shimbun,* March 4, 1980, p. 1.

30. "Otaiba Sekiyu Doryoku O Yakusoku," *Asahi Shimbun,* February 21, 1980, p. 1.

31. "Tainichi Sekiyu Zoryo O Keizoku," *Asahi Shimbun,* February 25, 1980, p. 1.

32. "Oman Enjo," *Asahi Shimbun,* February 26, 1980, p. 2.

33. "Shiriya-gawa Kakudai Yokyu," *Asahi Shimbun,* February 28, 1980, p. 2.

34. "Israel Tettai Jitsugen," *Asahi Shimbun,* March 3, 1980, p. 2, and "Yamani-shi Sonoda Tokushi Ni Genmei," *Asahi Shimbun,* March 5, 1980, p. 2.

35. "Suzuki Says U.S. Did Not Consult on Ending Grain Embargo," *New York Times,* April 29, 1981, p. 7.

36. Okita, *Economisuto Gaiso,* p. 33.

37. Interview with Tsutsumi.

38. "Bonn and Tokyo Resist Call for More Spending," *New York Times,* March 27, 1981, p. 7.

39. "Boei Chakujitsu Wa Doryoku," *Asahi Shimbun,* May 1, 1981, p. 2.

40. Ibid.

41. "Anpo Joyaku Kara Togen," *Asahi Shimbun* (evening edition), May 13, 1981, p. 1.

42. "Gaimusho Jimu Tokyoku Wa Konwaku," *Asahi Shimbun,* May 13, 1981, p. 2.

5 The Iran-Iraq War

*I expect this war to continue for several more months, a year or maybe
longer with the only big change being the [number of] casualties. . . .
It is most tragic, not just for the nations concerned, but also for the IJPC.*
—Koichi Tsutsumi, former deputy director of the Middle East and
Southwest Asia Bureau, Ministry of Foreign Affairs[1]

The Iran-Iraq war cut deeply into a vital part of Japan's Middle East
diplomacy. Tokyo officials, viewing Teheran as a pivotal point in Persian Gulf security, had worked to shield it through policies that would
contain the hostage crisis and deter the Soviet Union. For senior Japanese planners, the risk of incurring diplomatic strain with the super-
powers had been accepted as a cost of keeping Iran intact.

The new external threat of September 1980 quickly complicated
this analysis, however. The need to stay neutral toward an intra-Arab
conflict and to deal with an Iranian government that was near collapse
imposed strong limitations on what Japan could do. Because of these
impediments to official action, Tokyo leaders had to rely largely on
informal means to protect their interests in the area. It was against this
background of concerns and constraints that they turned to the Iran-
Japan Petrochemical Company (IJPC).

For decision makers in the Ministries of Foreign Affairs, Finance,
and International Trade and Industry, the joint venture represented
Tokyo's strongest link to leaders in Teheran as well as Japan's largest
overseas investment. The start of fighting on September 24 stirred
anxiety that the IJPC, located only sixty miles from the front, might
fall victim to military strikes. These fears soon became a policy nightmare when Iraqi planes attacked the project at least six times, causing
major damage to plant and pipeline facilities.

In Tokyo, doubts about whether the project could be salvaged
ignited a debate that pitted Mitsui, the principal private backer, against
the government. In early November, expected higher costs resulting
from time delays and structural repairs caused Mitsui to favor a pullout.
In the company's estimate, it could absorb the financial losses of withdrawal for two or three years and then count on Import-Export Bank
insurance to indemnify it for 70 percent of its IJPC debts.[2]

Tokyo refused to yield, however. Arguing that acts of war were not grounds for payment and criticizing Mitsui for what it said was shortsightedness, the government obtained the company's reluctant pledge to complete the project. Senior government officials felt that they had no choice; in their view, the diplomatic costs of withdrawal were too great.

Planners in the three ministries were convinced that dropping the IJPC would irreparably damage Japan's position in Iran and throughout the Middle East. In mid-November, a meeting between Iranian Prime Minister Mohammad Ali Rajai and a top Mitsui executive reminded Tokyo of the diplomatic importance of this "monument to the Revolution." Joined by his oil minister, the Iranian leader reiterated that "completion of the project was both the firm policy of [his] cabinet and the will of the people." Had Rajai, instead, indicated his government's desire to end the project, several key leaders in Japan would have gladly concurred, concluding that abandonment of this high-risk financial venture would not impair relations with Iran. The prime minister's insistence on continuing, however, meant that the IJPC would have to be revived.[3]

Further influencing the decision to recommit was the Soviet Union. Since the invasion of Afghanistan, officials in all three Japanese ministries had been concerned with increasing Soviet interest in Iran. Reported overtures to Teheran, including an offer of military assistance on October 5, seemed to underscore Moscow's wish to gain a foothold there. Should Mitsui unilaterally withdraw from the joint venture, senior government officials feared, Teheran would accuse Japan of bad-faith bargaining and would invite the Soviets into the country for technical help and financial assistance. Clearly, Tokyo felt that a Russian presence in Iran was in neither Japan's interests nor those of the West.

The final diplomatic incentive for staying with the project had more to do with other actors in the Gulf area. Within MITI and the other two ministries, there was an assessment that the hostage crisis had further circumscribed U.S. ability to operate in the Middle East. Since Japan could look even less to its closest ally for protection, it would have to be even more sensitive to the conditions and expectations of the region.[4]

In that regard, the IJPC seemed to be an economic investment with two symbolic edges. Bureaucratic planners believed that a decision to withdraw would undercut Tokyo's interests by transforming the project into "a monument of Japanese noncooperation throughout the Middle East." A decision to proceed, however, would help ensure stable oil supplies by signaling producer states that Japan could be trusted.

In Tokyo, what made this triangular relationship among petroleum, Arab goodwill, and the IJPC most apparent was the Iran-Iraq war itself.

For senior officials, the conflict emphasized Japan's inability to diversify its sources of oil supply and to shift away from its dependence on the Middle East. During the second half of 1980, Japan signed new oil-delivery agreements with Saudi Arabia and the United Arab Emirates to cover the shortfall that resulted from Japan's rejection, in April, of Iranian price demands and the disruption of Iraqi supplies in September. Third-quarter and fourth-quarter increases in deliveries from both Gulf States not only raised their share of Japan's total oil imports from 37 percent to 52 percent but also sharpened Japanese awareness of the need for allies in the area.[5]

To maintain access to their energy zone, planners in MITI, the Finance Ministry, and the Ministry of Foreign Affairs believed they would have to rely more on economic arrangements that might elicit friendship in the Arab world generally, and particularly from the Saudis. In Tokyo's view, Riyadh's traditional role as a 30 percent supplier of Japanese oil and its proven ability to raise that total quickly during crisis made it the prime target of investment diplomacy. Japanese decisions in late 1980 revealed the greater use of financial means to win favor with the Saudi government.

Before the war, Saudi Arabia had vaguely asked Tokyo for help in developing the heavy-industries part of its five-year, $250 billion modernization plan. On behalf of Prime Minister Zenko Suzuki, Foreign Minister Masayoshi Itoh and MITI Minister Rokusuke Tanaka had given a favorable response. Then Saudi leaders, evidently wishing to pin down Japan, asked Tokyo in November for help in completing a petrochemical project already backed by the Mitsubishi Group, Dow Chemical, and Riyadh. In December, the Japanese informally said yes. In April 1981, they officially designated that venture a national project, thus qualifying it for a $100 million subsidy from the Overseas Economic Development Fund.[6]

The assistance was given in part to calm the Mitsubishi Group, which had become quite nervous about Saudi demands that it and Dow assume a greater share of the costs.[7] To the three ministries, however, the foremost reason was more political than economic. According to one official:

> The whole Japanese investment is not necessary from a financial point of view. . . . Certainly, the Saudis have enough money to make this project feasible on their own. . . . What they wanted was a commitment from the Japanese Government and Japanese industry . . . to train a sufficient number of people in running a modern factory.[8]

For the Japanese, the emphasis "on close relations through economic cooperation was the common denominator of both the IJPC and the Saudi [petrochemical] project.[9] They therefore chose to push ahead on the joint venture in Iran, believing, in part, that withdrawal would erode Riyadh's confidence in Japan.

In addition to this tangle of diplomatic considerations, there also appeared to be a human element in the decision regarding the IJPC. In the Finance Ministry and particularly in MITI, senior planners seemed to have a strong personal stake in the success of the Iranian project. Although they were worried about how much more the venture would cost to complete, they were most concerned about what the loss would be if the IJPC should fail. Certainly, a large part of that loss would be the $1.8 billion investment of the 20 banks, 105 companies, and 2 government agencies that backed the venture. Evidently more than that, however, decision makers in MITI and the Finance Ministry were appalled at the prospect of seeing their hard work tossed away abruptly.

Since the first suspension of the project in March 1979, they had negotiated with Iranian leaders, committed money from the national treasury, argued with the United States, and chastised the Soviet Union in order to resurrect and protect the IJPC. With construction on the remaining 15 percent of facilities again under way, Tokyo had sent Naohiro Amaya to the Middle East in late September 1980 to reassure Mitsui of the government's continuing support and to help pave the way for a ceremony that would dedicate the venture in late November. Then, several days after the Amaya trip, Japanese officials blinked in disbelief as they saw those efforts tumble into a second suspension.[10] Clearly, the start of the war stunned them. Until February 1982, they struggled to keep the project alive.

In October 1980, bureaucratic planners first tried to preserve two resources that were crucial to the success of the joint venture. Under instructions from MITI and the Finance Ministry, the Overseas Economic Development Fund blocked monthly payments of $6 million to $8 million to Mitsui for work on the IJPC. To both ministries, this decision was strictly economic. One source explained:

> In September the IJPC had already been hit once, and we didn't want to pour money into something that might be damaged in the future. After all, that money belongs to our people . . . to the Japanese taxpayers . . . and we can use it again only when we are completely certain that the project will be safe [from attack].[11]

Next, Tokyo leaders and Mitsui agreed to withdraw the 750 Japanese nationals from the construction site on October 14. Iranian Prime Minister Rajai, President Bani-Sadr, and other officials did not object.

They evidently made several demands, however, to assure themselves of a continuing Japanese commitment to the project. In Teheran, Mitsui Vice-President Hideaki Yamashita responded for his company and the government, promising to have his men return to work once their safety could be guaranteed and further pledging to send Iran nearly $250,000 a day for wages that Japanese business had originally agreed to pay.[12]

Finally, the Japanese took a more direct approach to the immediate threat. On October 17, Foreign Minister Ito met a special emissary from the Iraqi government. During a one hour, forty minute session, the foreign minister reiterated Japan's complete neutrality toward the conflict as well as its strong desire for an early ceasefire. Ito also asked Iraq to support the right of safe passage for sea traffic through the Straight of Hormuz and the Shatt-al-Arab waterway. Trying to stand midway between Baghdad and the IJPC, he indicated Tokyo's willingness to help repair Japanese projects damaged in Iraq and its wish for an end to the attacks against the venture in Iran.[13]

Parallel to this initial flurry of activity was an assessment of the war that would shape subsequent Japanese policy toward the IJPC. At the start of fighting, the Japanese judged that Baghdad held the overwhelming strategic edge. Not only was its air force qualitatively and quantitatively superior, but its war effort was free from the fissures in military command and political leadership that threatened to crack Iran's counteroffensive.[14] What Tokyo foresaw, however, did not occur.

Instead of ending with lightning charges by Iraq, the conflict dissipated into a series of erratic and indecisive attacks. Although there were punitive strikes against Teheran, Abadan, and other cities, Baghdad forces seemed to be content, in October and November, to consolidate their gains along the 500-mile front. The strongest evidence of restraint appeared to be the Iraqi decision not to push into the Khuzistan Province, the source of Iran's oil.

In Tokyo, several officials attributed this unexpected turn of events to the surprise showing of Iran's military. Other, more central decision makers, however, gave their explanation a political emphasis. According to them, Iraqi President Saddam Hussein had wanted to regain control over the Shatt-al-Arab waterway, three islands in the Strait of Hormuz, and other disputed territories in a way that would not perpetuate the animosity of the Iranian people. These planners believed that the Iraqi leader was after all a member of the Arab League and wished to avoid a permanent conflict with Iran and other countries in the region.[15] To Hussein's surprise, however, Ayatollah Ruhollah Khomeini proved to be more stubborn than originally had been anticipated. Rather than accepting Hussein's peace proposals in late September or acknowledging the mediation efforts of Pakistani President Mohammed Zia-ul-Haq and PLO Chairman Yasir Arafat in early October, the Iranian leader had vowed that his country would fight until the end.

Because of the cap on further escalation, Hussein apparently had chosen to wait for his frail opponent to die and to see what would happen politically in Teheran after that. This strategy, Japanese logic seemed to indicate, would place Baghdad in a favorable position by allowing it to strike a bargain with a less rigid regime or to recapture territory from a more divided foe. To Tokyo officials, the implication of this assessment was painfully clear. Iraq's pursuit of limited objectives with limited force had yielded a war of indeterminable length.

In Japan, the need to brace the IJPC for indefinite suspension soon touched off another round of infighting between Mitsui and the government. On November 28, representatives of the Iran Chemical Development Company (ICDC), the Japanese half of the joint venture, met with MITI Minister Rokusuke Tanaka. At that time, Hideaki Yamashita, ICDC president and Mitsui vice-president, spoke for the group, painting a bleak picture of its financial future.[16]

The present arrangement with Iran, he emphasized, required that the ICDC send the IJPC $54 million between late October and late December. The three monthly installments would cover wages and interest on domestic loans that the ICDC had secured for the project. As the parent company, the IJPC would keep the wage part of the payment and remit the interest portion to supporting banks in Japan. What troubled the ICDC, according to Yamashita, was the shutoff of government assistance from the Overseas Economic Development Fund when the war broke out. That money had been vital, since it had represented 40 percent, or $22 million, of the total amount owed by the ICDC for the final quarter of 1980.

Although the ICDC had scraped together enough to cover the $6.8 million lost in October, it would be unable to do that again in late November. Yamashita explained that the resources were simply not there. The ICDC president therefore offered two alternatives that would free his group from its financial bind. In Yamashita's view, the government should reverse the present policy by turning on the tap of the Overseas Economic Development Fund. Failing that, Tokyo should lessen the ICDC's burden by allowing it to defer the interest-payment part of monies sent to the IJPC until the war ended.[17]

During subsequent meetings, ICDC and Mitsui executives made the same case with slight variations. On December 4, Yamashita told Chief Cabinet Secretary Kiichi Miyazawa that Iranian law gave priority to wage payments in contractual relations. He therefore concluded that interest payments were the only area in which the ICDC could make the reductions needed to keep it solvent. Then, on December 17, the director of Mitsui Heavy Industries, Nariakira Ikeda, presented his list of financial woes to MITI Minister Tanaka. The Japanese executive first repeated the earlier refrain of the difficulties arising from lost government revenue. What made this situation worse, he added, was the inability of the ICDC to trim its operating expenses by a proportionate amount. Because of this economic crunch, the ICDC would have to ask for Tokyo's help in covering the unpaid portion of the bill for construction performed so far. Moreover, the group would need the government's good offices in persuading Japanese banks to delay the due dates for interest payments on outstanding loans.[18]

Senior planners in both MITI and the Finance Ministry reacted with strong displeasure. They continued to believe that Tokyo could not reextend aid from the Overseas Economic Development Fund while the war was still in progress. Moreover, they were skeptical of Mitsui's arguments. In their view, the assertions of financial setback seemed to imply something else.

MITI and Finance Ministry officials believed that Mitsui had originally undertaken the project in October 1971 as a result of good-faith bargaining with the Iranian government. Political changes and Moslem revolution notwithstanding, they felt that Mitsui had the duty to keep its word so long as there was a chance of success. From the perspective of the two ministries, the requests for government support amounted to attempts by Mitsui to shirk its corporate responsibility. As one official related: "The project is Mitsui's. And as such it should unequivocally state that it will see the IJPC through till completion or the failure [of the joint venture] is no longer in question."[19]

Casting further doubt on Mitsui's intentions was the second half of its solution. The suggestion to defer interest payments angered several senior government officials, apparently causing one of them to wonder aloud whether anyone in Mitsui understood finance. For Tokyo, sliding back the due dates violated the fundamental principle of the financial world. "Interest," one decision-maker reiterated, "is where lending institutions make their profit." He and others feared that acceptance of Mitsui's demand would place them "in a very uncertain, very difficult position." Such action not only would raise questions about resorting to interest deferral again but also would open the possibility of making additional loans to Mitsui interest-free.[20]

Aside from these distant concerns, there was a more immediate reason for standing firm. From a financial point of view, Japanese loans were the lynchpins of the entire project. In a complex set of four separate arrangements, the Import-Export Bank, 20 private banks, and 100 Japanese companies had provided $980 million to Mitsui and the ICDC for the IJPC. In addition, the Import-Export Bank and 20 companies had extended another $380 million to the Foreign Ministry of Iran and the National Petrochemical Company of Iran (NPC)—the Iranian counterpart of the ICDC—thus exposing Japanese institutions in total loan commitments of $1.36 billion. The second largest source of capital, loans floated on the Eurodollar market by the NPC, came to $900 million. Running a distant third were direct Japanese investments of $302 million by Mitsui, the ICDC, the Overseas Economic Development Fund, and 100 Japanese companies.[21] In this context, it was unthinkable that two of the smallest contributors should be allowed to tinker with the financial structure in a way that could cause it to collapse. Clearly, Mitsui and the ICDC would have to pay their interest.

Though taking a hardline attitude on this issue, MITI and Finance Ministry planners were willing to show some flexibility in considering other, more reasonable forms of help. The solutions and scenarios they devised were divided according to time. As the longest-term concern, the question of post—Iran-Iraq war policy loomed the largest. During the first half of 1981, decision makers started discussions with all Japanese parties involved in the project. As one official explained:

> We would of course like to have the IJPC proceed and contribute to good relations with Iran. This is most desirable. . . . We are therefore talking to Mitsui and the other Japanese investors about various aspects of the project. Instead of focusing narrowly on the damage inflicted to the facilities, we are considering how many times over the original estimate the project will cost to complete . . . what needs to be done and whether new money will necessarily lead to success.[22]

Although those joint reviews were conducted in secret, they evidently were guided by three ruling assumptions. First, Mitsui and the ICDC would have to look largely to private lenders for capital to cover Japan's share of the $450 million to $1.2 billion in additional costs. Second, both organizations could proceed with construction only when the government was satisfied that peace between Iran and Iraq was real. Third, they would be allowed to withdraw from the IJPC in the event that Tokyo and/or Teheran concluded that the venture was no longer financially feasible.

A second set of policies sharpened by MITI and the Finance Ministry targeted a more tangible concern. In the view of both bureaucracies, all business activity on the project had been suspended. As a matter of economic equity, Mitsui and the ICDC had the right to curtail their business expenses. The question was how.

In the first half of 1981, the Finance Ministry proposed one possibility that emphasized the other side of loan repayment. Under the original agreement, Mitsui and the ICDC would complete interest payments and begin principal payments in February 1982. Finance Ministry officials believed that rescheduling the principal payments should be considered if the conflict lasted beyond 1981. According to one source:

> Extending the payment and the return of the principal has very little to do with the relationship between earnings and expenses. Suspending the interest is of course another story.[23]

Complementing this decision was a separate attempt to plug unnecessary capital outflows from Mitsui and the ICDC. In the view of senior government planners, about one-third of each month's payment to the IJPC was being squandered as wages for work on a project that had come to a halt. Despite this situation, the provision in the original agreement that stipulated a fixed, construction-cost split with Iran still remained in effect. In late February 1981, representatives from MITI and Mitsui apparently agreed on a strategy that would bring expenditures and obligations into a more realistic balance. From late April, it was decided, Mitsui and the ICDC could stop their monthy transfers to the IJPC. Nevertheless, both organizations would have to make their monthly interest payments directly to the various lending institutions in Japan.[24] For MITI and Mitsui, the net effect was a minus in unnecessary labor costs.

Following this consensus on a new framework of financing, MITI and Mitsui leaders evidently decided that ICDC President Yamashita should travel to Teheran. The purpose of that trip would be to explain the Tokyo-Mitsui decision to Iranian leaders and to reassure them of his group's commitment to the IJPC.

After arriving in Teheran on March 4, Yamashita met with President Bani-Sadr and leaders of the NPC. The Japanese executive started the discussion by reaffirming his intention to complete the IJPC master plan. Bani-Sadr then spoke, expressing concern over spiraling construction costs and mentioning his wish to send an economic mission to Tokyo for a review of the situation with the Japanese government. The Iranian president also stressed his optimism that the war would end in two months and suggested that a team of Japanese technicians be dispatched to survey the damage. Fearing for the safety of these technicians, Yamashita said no. In his view, such action could be contemplated only when peace had been established and the team's freedom of movement could be guaranteed.

In addition to these comments, the ICDC president broached the

Japanese plan to stop future payments to the joint venture. It was apparently at this time that Bani-Sadr agreed. The Iranian president and other Teheran officials had already concluded that the costs of construction needed to be checked. Unlike Japan, which had only a skeleton crew in Bandar Khomeini, Iran had kept its 1,500 workers on the construction site. Despite the ICDC's 50 percent contribution to wages, Teheran was having difficulty providing its half of construction costs. Indeed, as Iranian leaders later admitted, the country would sink deeper into economic trouble if it were required to carry its full obligations on the IJPC.[25] Evidently during the session with Yamashita, Bani-Sadr also probed the possibility of restarting monies from the Overseas Economic Development Fund. Further, he said that Teheran would similarly freeze its construction account and eventually repay its wages on a retroactive basis.

Several months later, the Iranian president confirmed parts of this agreement and repeated his demands in a roundabout manner. In an interview with the Japanese press on May 1, he assiduously avoided attacks on the April 23 announcement by Yamashita that direct funding to the IJPC would be suspended. Referring to the wartime situation, Bani-Sadr indicated his understanding of the ICDC's position and decision. He added that, though he lacked the authority to discuss the IJPC with Tokyo leaders, he doubted whether private industry alone could shoulder the Japanese half of the project. Of course, Bani-Sadr emphasized, his country would continue to underwrite its share of the costs and fully expected Japanese workers to return as soon as the conflict ended.

Having obtained Iran's assent to a reduction of project expenditures, leaders in Tokyo and at Mitsui began to grapple with a general problem that would directly affect the IJPC. Throughout the spring and summer, bureaucratic and business planners watched helplessly as the Moslem revolution entered a new, even more chaotic phase. From mid-April, it appeared that the political standing of Bani-Sadr was starting to slip. Reports of the president's infighting with the clergy-dominated government, Khomeini's criticism of politicians challenging Islamic authority, and the removal of Bani-Sadr's associates from high office suggested that a change of power was imminent.

On June 22, speculation became reality when the religious leader relieved the Iranian president of his duties as commander-in-chief of the armed forces. Fearing for his life, Bani-Sadr went underground and one month later hijacked an airplane from Teheran to France. During that four-week interval, Iran was further convulsed by other events, including the continuation of "revolutionary court" executions, which reportedly raised the post-Shah death toll to 1,600 and the bombing of the ruling Islamic Republican Party headquarters, which killed Chief Justice Ayatollah Mohammed Behesti and thirty-two other senior politicians.

For ranking Japanese officials, this situation presented an uncomfortable dilemma. The toppling of Iranian leaders by death threat and murder dramatically reinforced the importance of the IJPC. In their view, it was the last remaining channel of goodwill with a government in which anarchy reigned supreme and the tools of diplomacy had been blunted. As one official lamented: "Japan has no other [major] options in keeping relations with Iran open. . . . The IJPC is it."[26]

At the same time, however, planners in Tokyo and at Mitsui judged that little could be done to safeguard the venture. They realized that much needed to be discussed with Teheran to prevent the project from folding. Ideally, negotiations should be conducted on such problems as the apportionment of additional expenses; the availability of natural gas, naphtha, and other raw materials; and profit-sharing on the petrochemicals themselves. Unfortunately, the wave of violence, which had underscored the significance of the project, had impeded the start of substantive talks that were vital to its future.

To Tokyo and Mitsui, there were two roadblocks to detailed discussions between Japanese business and Iranian representatives. They first feared that the post–Bani-Sadr administration might not last. Certainly, Tokyo and Mitsui knew that guarantees on political longevity could be neither requested nor made. Nevertheless, they wanted to have reasonable confidence that the parties with whom Japan bargained would stay alive and in power.[27]

Further preventing the formation of joint solutions was the matter of a new leadership itself. In the opinion of Tokyo and Mitsui, the specter of disorderly succession meant that any agreements concluded with one set of Iranian decision makers might be abandoned by their replacement. Thus, whatever was finalized at a given moment would have to be confirmed and possibly renegotiated from scratch with a new regime.

For Mitsui in particular, subsequent events only reinforced these anxieties. In late July, its representatives traveled to Teheran for exploratory meetings with Iranian officials. On July 27, 28, and 29, they pushed hard for a general principle that presumably would guide future negotiations with a more stable government. During those sessions, they proposed revision of the present arrangement, which called for a fifty-fifty expenditure split with the NPC. Failure to do so, the Japanese argued, would undermine the project by unfairly straddling Mitsui and the ICDC with large losses that were not of their own making. Iranian representatives objected, however. In their view, the Iran-Iraq war had not invalidated the terms of the original contract. Therefore, what had been decided before the conflict still remained in effect.[28]

Unable to establish their basic position, ICDC President Yamashita and the other Japanese representatives returned to Tokyo, where four weeks later they received news of the deaths of President Rajai and Prime Minister Bahonar. This, they initially believed, was the final straw. From Mitsui's perspective, continuing instability had combined with recent doubts to ensure the futility of any discussions with Iran. On August 31, Mitsui President Toshikuni Yahiro, referring to the political and economic downturn in Iran, stated that his company could no longer cope with the situation there.

Although they shared Mitsui's concerns until the assassinations, MITI officials took a different position after them. Political uncertainties, they judged, would naturally hamper commercial talks between Mitsui and the NPC, but that alone did not justify abandoning the joint venture. Indeed, Iran's strong pressure in September for a round of meetings apparently meant that negotiations would have to proceed, for better or for worse. As a result, MITI planners implemented two sets of policies to bring Mitsui to the bargaining table.

Formally, they clarified the ground rules regarding payment on the Import-Export Bank insurance policy that covered $600 million of Mitsui's outstanding debt. To MITI, such considerations as a pullout by Iran or a withdrawal of Japanese banks would influence any decision on indemnification. The decision maker would be MITI, however, not Mitsui. In MITI's judgment, payment was still premature.

Informally, MITI transmitted the same message in more vivid terms. In an off-the-record conversation, MITI leaders told Mitsui that withdrawal was out of the question. Only "an act of God" would release the company from its commercial obligation, and that, in MITI's view, meant a disclaimer from Iran. Naturally, Tokyo would be willing to indemnify Mitsui if the Islamic republic should leave the project, citing the war with Iraq or its inability to uphold the terms of the original contract. Such a situation would never occur, however, for the Imam's petrochemical project, as it was known in Iran, had become both a political test and a diplomatic commitment of the current regime. The term *Imam,* in this context, refers to the Ayatollah Khomeini. In this sense, a decision to quit would be a self-inflicted wound on the revolution itself.[29]

Given Teheran's participation as a constant, MITI officials acknowledged a different, more difficult reality. The Iran-Iraq war—the major threat to the project—showed no signs of ending. Initially, MITI officials assumed that Teheran would be unable to undertake a prolonged struggle, since supply and arms shortages would eventually force a surrender. That did not happen, however. The reason, from the ministry's perspective, appeared to be a different concept of war held in the Middle East. While emphasizing cultural differences between Japan and Iran, and what they considered their ignorance of "Islamic feeling," MITI officials predicted that a protracted fight lay ahead. As one planner observed, in "normal" nation-against-nation conflicts, one side makes a deep thrust toward the other's capital, thus causing his opponent to "throw up his own hands in defeat." In the absence of such actions, the Iran-Iraq war would continue.

Oddly enough, however, future uncertainty made MITI's immediate policy even clearer. Until a total surrender or bona fide ceasefire evolved, the IJPC would have to stay in deep freeze. Meanwhile, MITI officials assured Mitsui, the government would do its best to ease the company's financial burden and make the project commercially feasible.

After poking Mitsui with their insurance stick and offering it a carrot of sorts, MITI planners soon dealt with the other half of the joint venture. On October 30, NPC President Mostafa Taheri arrived for a week of talks with government and business leaders. To MITI officials, their own session, scheduled for November 2, would be crucial.

Within the bureaucracy, there was a feeling that the IJPC was at a crossroads. In the first half of 1981, senior Japanese officials had done what they could domestically to keep the venture afloat. With the refinancing arrangements in Japan completed, IJPC planners would have to take the next step into economic areas that could make or break the project. That, however, would require the cooperation of Iran. Unless Japan's partner was willing to do what it could, there appeared to be little point in proceeding. As one decision maker related: "It is ridiculous to continue with a project that is bound to fail for economic reasons . . . [since] such a project will contribute to absolutely nothing."[30]

Specifically, MITI officials felt that the meeting with Taheri must accomplish three interrelated objectives. First, the technical problems would have to be addressed. Of these problems, raw materials seemed to be the most important; as one planner remarked, it was only "common sense." To MITI, the success of any petrochemical project depended on the price and availability of the required natural resources. For the IJPC, however, the financial calculations on these items had been made at the time of the Shah; since then, much had changed.

Particularly disturbing was the oil-production dropoff of at least 49 percent that had occurred under Islamic rule. As one official related: "The whole structure of the IJPC rests on the premise of free fuel . . . that is, the gas that is emitted when petroleum is pumped out of the ground." Adding to this uncertainty was the situation regarding naphtha and other vital ingredients. With Abadan and other production centers under Iraqi attack, key Japanese decision makers doubted Teheran's ability to meet either the nonenergy or the energy half of the project's needs. As a result, two questions would have to be put to the NPC president: How could these shortfalls be filled? and What would it cost to fill them?

Besides this resource issue, the meeting with Taheri must consider a second technical item. In fairness to Mitsui, Iran would now have to shoulder the additional expenses of the project. According to MITI's assessment, Mitsui had hit a financial wall. Not only did it lack the resources to pay the reconstruction costs resulting from the war, but it also would be squeezed in the future by shrinking profits on petrochemicals, whose market prices had steadily declined.[31]

For objective reasons, MITI planners were optimistic that Teheran would agree eventually. Once the war ended, it was assumed, both combatants would seek aid from abroad and, perhaps, reparations from each other. With regard to Iran, Islamic leaders would look to Mitsui as an important component in their recovery effort. Before submitting their needs to Tokyo and the company, however, they would first have to determine what was lost. In so doing, they would naturally view the damage done to the IJPC as part of their responsibility, not Mitsui's.

Finally, MITI leaders wanted to impress upon Taheri what was most obvious to them. The IJPC was, after all, a commercial venture. Though backing it politically, Tokyo could do little to make the project succeed financially. For that, Iran would have to depend on itself and its corporate partner.

The message of this position and the earlier two statements was implicit but clear. Taheri and other Iranian officials had two choices. Either they could work constructively with Mitsui in forging solutions to the problems confronting the IJPC, or they could watch helplessly as the Japanese withdrew.

With their stances thus decided, MITI planners waited for the NPC president. Before that meeting, however, they heard something that was disheartening. They received an oral summary from the ICDC of a so-called feasibility study that Taheri had brought with him to Japan. The document, a review of such topics as the raw material situation in Iran and the profit margin of the project, concluded that the IJPC would be a major success. Especially worrisome to ministry planners was the statistical basis of the study. Using numbers from the pre–Iran-Iraq war period, it indicated that Teheran had not yet considered the economics of the new situation.[32] What followed on the afternoon of November 2 was most disappointing.

During the meeting with Taheri, MITI representatives got to the point quickly. While underscoring their understanding of Teheran's political position, they emphasized the need to make the project commercially profitable. Part of that, they continued, required a scientific evaluation by Teheran of the IJPC as it then existed. Without such information, the venture would fail. To reemphasize that message, MITI planners also made their own item-by-item review of the various natural resources, telling the NPC president just how grim the situation was.[33]

This effort notwithstanding, the MITI representatives lacked confidence that their message was getting through. Taheri's responses to their questions seemed to be evasive. More troublesome, though, was a creeping uncertainty about the translator. Since neither side spoke the other's language, they had agreed to communicate through a third party, who could interpret the English comments of the MITI planners and the Persian statements of the Iranian official. Several minutes into the session, it appeared to the Japanese that much of what they and Taheri said was being needlessly omitted; the two groups spoke at great length, but what came back in translation seemed to be "too short, too simple."[34]

The upshot of all this was a series of general impressions. Taheri and his colleagues, MITI planners judged, had not come to grips with the realities of the IJPC. In the extreme, it seemed that Teheran was quite willing to supply the raw materials free, but that was impossible. So long as this absence of analysis persisted, MITI could neither project future costs nor formulate the policies that might ensure financial feasibility. In short, Iran's nonposition played havoc with Japanese calculations.

Despite this dismal state of affairs, there apparently was one cause for hope. Taheri and the other Iranians were still firmly committed to the IJPC. The difficulty for them, MITI planners judged, had been a political environment that precluded a calm review of objective economic factors. Indeed, in the view of Tokyo officials, the Iranians had so far kept their word regarding their half of the joint venture. Most important, they had promptly paid all monies owed under the current contract. Nothing in the November 2 meeting suggested that Iranian integrity should now be doubted. Accordingly, MITI planners seemed to feel that, in time, Taheri and his superiors might be persuaded to take a no-nonsense approach to the project. What was needed, therefore, was a firm but patient hand by Mitsui at the bargaining table. Unfortunately, the chance of that were rapidly fading.

On November 3 and 4, Taheri met with ranking Mitsui executives. To the Iranian's apparent surprise, the session was much rougher than he had expected. In caustic terms, the businessmen said that the Moslem revolution and the Iran-Iraq war might have already undone the joint venture. With regard to the feasibility study, they implied that it meant nothing. In their view, the document failed to provide credible answers to their resource questions. Moreover, it did not close the gap between Iran's conservative $2 billion estimate of yearly petrochemical sales and Mitsui's own high figure of $1 billion.[35]

Then, one day later, Mitsui executives turned on the bargaining heat. Meeting with Taheri on November 5, they flatly refused his earlier request to continue negotiations in Teheran. Next, they issued an ultimatum. According to them, further discussions on raw materials, profit, and other key details would be pointless unless the NPC first agreed to bear the additional costs of the project. They emphasized that Mitsui would of course be willing to provide construction assistance on a cost-plus-fee basis, but Iran must accept, by December 15, full responsibility for all rebuilding.[36]

The reason for this assertiveness from Mitsui appeared to be a belief that the time for a showdown had finally come. From the company's perspective, a deadline would provide two attractive alternatives. Refusal by the NPC would mean Iranian withdrawal and insurance money, whereas acceptance would mean Iranian money and possible IJPC success. To MITI, however, the ultimatum symbolized something slightly different.

Until November 5, ministry planners had to deal with two Mitsuis: one group that had reluctantly backed the IJPC and another that had strongly opposed it. Within the company, it was felt, the two elements had engaged in a bitter personal battle, resulting in a breakdown in policy consensus. MITI planners judged that the individuals advocating pullout, unable to have their own way, had tried to apply external pressure on the company and on Tokyo through the news media. By developing contacts with journalists of the *Asahi Shimbun* and other national dailies, these dissidents had been partly responsible for two inaccurate stories on the joint venture.

On April 24, 1981, the Japanese press had reported the suspension of ICDC payments to the IJPC, interpreting it as an indication of a forthcoming withdrawal by Mitsui. On September 2, the newspapers had characterized a speech by MITI Minister Rokusuke Tanaka as a government decision to abandon the project. Though exasperated, MITI officials evidently felt that direct intervention into the company's internal affairs would be inappropriate. In their view, their only recourse was to call in the Japanese journalists and explain to them why participation was inevitable.

The Mitsui ultimatum of November 5, however, indicated that a major change had occurred. From MITI's perspective, Mitsui's statement revealed that the company as a whole had become more realistic. Concluding that the project was no longer worth the commercial risks, the dominant group of executives had cast aside their former belief in its symbolic importance. Under the rules of indemnification, however, they would need Iran's help in obtaining the insurance monies that would minimize company losses. By burdening the NPC with heavy expenses and a short response period, Mitsui leaders judged they might force Teheran to quit and thus secure the required release. In MITI's view, it was a blatant display of brinksmanship.

As the company and Tokyo would soon learn, however, the Iranians were not about to blink. On November 26, a cabinet-level Iranian committee initially indicated a decision to stay with the project. Paradoxically, the reason may have been the very absence of economic analysis that MITI planners had earlier lamented. By Teheran's own admission, the country's gross national product had plummeted 33 percent between 1978 and 1980. Despite the transfer of overseas assets following the hostage crisis, Iran's foreign exchange reserves of $10 billion in November 1979 had fallen below $4 billion in March 1981.[37] Because of this weak balance sheet, the IJPC appeared to be a luxury that Iran could ill afford.

More directly, information on Teheran's policymaking, though fragmentary, suggests that economic factors were given short shrift. Within the Iranian government, one person who had studied both Mitsui's ultimatum and the financial situation spoke out against greater participation. On December 7, the minister of public utilities advocated a formal withdrawal, arguing that soaring costs had simply made the IJPC unfeasible. Official reaction in Teheran was quick. The NPC president immediately dismissed this as one person's opinion and reaffirmed the government's intention to finish the joint venture. At the same time, though, Taheri continued to sidestep Mitsui's demand, saying that the IJPC could succeed under the present fifty-fifty cost-sharing arrangement.[38]

Then, on December 8, Teheran evidently blended this willingness to complete the project and the uncertainty over the economics involved in a response that accepted the ultimatum, but on terms that did not accept it. The first two parts of the reply were straightforward statements emphasizing Iran's determination to stand behind the IJPC and the importance it placed on Japanese cooperation. In Mitsui's view, however, the third part was uncomfortably vague. It stipulated that, while agreeing to the principle of payment for all expenses, Iran needed to know how high the ceiling on construction costs would go. By this language, Iran had made its acceptance not only unclear but also subject to further negotiations with Japan.

Mitsui leaders were not pleased. During his unofficial visit to Teheran on December 11, Yamashita tried to pry loose a detailed explanation of what part three of the Iranian response meant. The ICDC president was unsuccessful. After returning to Tokyo on December 16, he and other Mitsui officers complained of the ambiguity that permeated Iran's response. Arguing that changed circumstances had effectively abrogated the present agreement, they concluded that another, more carefully drafted ultimatum should be sent to Iran. That document, Mitsui believed, would narrow Teheran's range of responses to a clear yes or no.

On December 28, Yamashita, Yahiro, and presidents of the ICDC member companies put together a three-point message for Teheran. The first point was their judgment that the destruction of conditions underlying the present agreement had rendered it ineffective. The second point acknowledged Iran's request for a statement on construction cost ceiling but added that the inability to survey the construction site would prevent an accurate estimate. The third part asked Iran to confirm Mitsui's understanding that part three of the earlier Iranian response had signaled a pledge to pay all expenses incurred since the start of the Iran-Iraq war. The Mitsui executives added one condition: Iran must send its new reply by January 8.

What they eventually received appeared to be a great disappointment. Saying only that Teheran still backed the IJPC, Iranian officials neither accepted nor rejected the company's new ultimatum. With January 8 fast approaching, Mitsui leaders extended the deadline to later in the month. Moreover, they demanded that the NPC agree to terminate the project if failed to recognize the ineffectiveness of the present contract by then.

On January 25, Teheran gave its formal reply. In an interview with the news media, the NPC president offered a $540 million loan to the IJPC. That money, Taheri explained, would be used to repair war damage and to complete the final phase of construction. Apparently to induce a positive response from Mitsui, other Iranian spokesmen assured the Japanese that the NPC would make good on its next regular payment, due in February. Of course, they added, a decision by Mitsui to quit would force them to begin legal proceedings in Iran's Supreme Court.[39]

At this point, MITI decided to step in. Among ranking bureaucrats, there were mixed emotions. They felt that Mitsui's ploy had come to an end. In their view, the loan offer had effectively eliminated the possibility of insurance monies, thus locking the company into a continuing relationship with Teheran. MITI planners were skeptical, however, about whether Iran had yet taken a hard look at what the project required. From their perspective, the $540 million represented part of a deep political commitment that lacked any basis in economic fact. How was this figure derived? Could Iran repay it? Would it cover all additional costs?

Unable to solve these and other puzzles on their own, MITI planners adopted a two-point position. They informed Mitsui that Tokyo would not respond to any request for indemnification. Accordingly, the company had little choice but to negotiate with the NPC and reach a realistic understanding on what needed to be done and what each side could do to make the project commercially profitable.

On February 23, representatives from the ICDC and NPC formally began a third round of discussions in Teheran. For the Japanese government, however, further action on the joint venture would have to wait until a common agreement was achieved. Nevertheless, the success of the IJPC and, more broadly, Japan's position in Iran and throughout the Middle East would ultimately hinge on other factors over which Tokyo had no control. The outcome of the Iran-Iraq war, the future of Teheran after Khomeini, and the final cost of the project were questions whose answers were murky at best and doubtful at worst. In this sense, the use of private business to protect Tokyo's interests in the area appeared to be foolish as well as futile. In another sense, however, it was the best that Japan could do.

Notes

1. Personal interview with Koichi Tsutsumi, former deputy director of the Middle East and Southwest Asia Bureau, Ministry of Foreign Affairs, July 17, 1981.

2. "Mitsui Bussan Iran Tettai Hakaru," *Asahi Shimbun,* November 9, 1980, p. 1.

3. Personal interview with a high-ranking Japanese official (hereafter cited as Source C), August 1982.

4. "Amaya, Iran Sekika Tettai O Hihan," *Asahi Shimbun,* November 18, 1980, p. 1; also, interviews with officials in the Foreign Ministry and Finance Ministry.

5. "Sauji Genyu No Tainichi Kyoryoku, Hitochiiki 50-pasento Ijo Ni Fuan Mo," *Asahi Shimbun,* November 21, 1980, p. 9, and "Sogo Anpo Kaigi Ga Shokaigo," *Asahi Shimbun,* December 2, 1980, p. 1.

6. Ministry of International Trade and Industry, *Keizai Kyoryoku No Genjo To Mondaiten, 1982* (Tokyo: Tsusho Sangyosho, 1982), p. 384.

7. Interview with Source C.

8. Interview with Tsutsumi.

9. Personal interview with a high-ranking Japanese official (hereafter cited as Source D), July 1981.

10. Interview with Source C.

11. Interview with Source D.

12. "Iran Sekika Kansei Tsuyoku Nozomo," *Asahi Shimbun,* November 18, 1980, p. 1.

13. "Horumuzu Kaiko Anzen Kakuho O Yosei, Iraku Tokushi No Gaiso," *Asahi Shimbun,* October 18, 1980, p. 1.

14. Interview with Source C.

15. Ibid.

16. "Iran Sekika De Mitsui Gurupu, Mazu Kongetsu 27-oku En," *Asahi Shimbun,* November 28, 1980, p. 1.

17. Ibid.

18. "Tsusanso To Bussan Baicho," *Asahi Shimbun,* December 20, 1980, p. 8.

19. Personal interview with a high-ranking Japanese official, July 1981.

20. Interview with Source D.

21. "Iran Sekika No Shuhen," *Asahi Shimbun,* December 10, 1980, p. 3.

22. Interview with Source D.

23. Ibid.

24. "Sukin Chushi O Kimeru," *Asahi Shimbun,* April 24, 1981, p. 1.

25. Interview with Source C.

26. Personal interview with a high-ranking Japanese official, August 1982.

27. Interview with Source C.

28. "Kihon Keiyaku Kaitei O Hitei," *Asahi Shimbun,* July 30, 1981, p. 9.

29. Interview with Source C.

30. Ibid.

31. Ibid.

32. Ibid.

33. Ibid.

34. Ibid.

35. "Key Japan-Iranian Deal Sours," *Washington Post,* November 22, 1981, pp. 26 and 27.

36. "Mitsui Iran-gawa Ni Kigen Tsuki," *Asahi Shimbun,* November 6, 1981, p. 1.

37. "Bani-Sadr Expresses Alarm on Economy," *New York Times,* April 6, 1981, p. 6.

38. "Doryokuso Ga Saisansei O Hitei, Taheri Sosai Wa Keizoku Shucho," *Asahi Shimbun,* December 8, 1981, p. 9.

39. "IJPC No Kojihi Futan," *Asahi Shimbun,* January 26, 1982, p. 8.

Appendix:
A Regional View of
World Politics

The Middle East is a practical problem with theoretical roots. Since 1945, the United States had presided as prime mover in Tokyo's diplomacy. Dependence on Washington for strategic protection and economic development led Japan, in the 1950s and throughout the 1960s, to embrace a strong pro-American posture in foreign affairs. Although there were sharp differences regarding security and trade-related matters, they could be compromised or at least tolerated so long as national survival was assured in a bilateral context. After 1973, however, that would no longer be possible.

The oil shock not only signaled the ability of producer states to determine oil production and oil price, but it also marked the emergence of a new actor, whose own difficulties directly threatened Japan and were beyond the control of the United States. On a basic level, it was the nonglobal nature of world politics that prodded and constrained Tokyo's subsequent approaches toward the Persian Gulf area.

When viewed from Japan, the international system appeared to be a matrix of country-to-country and country-to-region relations that arose and transformed over time in response to strategic, economic, and political concerns that arose and transformed over time. The diplomatic picture that developed, therefore, was an inner circle of cross-national and cross-area alliances that shifted according to shifts in external functional stimuli.

In the mid-1970s and early 1980s, the Japanese stood between two matrices—one that had been wrapped around the United States and one that must include the Middle East. Unlike ongoing realignments with Communist China and Southeast Asia, a direct move toward the Gulf area would intersect an opposing set of U.S. policies. To avoid entanglements with Washington while treating the problems in the Persian Gulf region, Tokyo officials had to weave a new pattern of diplomacy. The result was a network of bilateral, multilateral, and transnational measures applied selectively to three Middle Eastern concerns.

Regime Instability

Political disorder was a constant fear for Tokyo officials. Plagued by ethnic division, factional infighting, and weak infrastructures, the governments of the Gulf area were generally thought to be fragile entities that could easily collapse. Crystallizing this anxiety between 1979 and 1982 was the situation in Iran.

From Tokyo's perspective, the overthrow of the Shah was the most far-reaching single development of the four-year period. Not only did the Moslem revolution eliminate the core element in Persian Gulf security, but it also implanted a leadership whose own turmoil appeared to impede moderate-Arab support of the Camp David accords, end U.S. influence in Teheran, induce the Soviet move into Afghanistan, and help precipitate Iraq's strike against Iran.

Given this ripple effect, the Japanese equated a less chaotic regime in Teheran with greater stability throughout the Middle East. As they also discovered, however, wishing and having were two very different things.

After late 1979, Japanese diplomatic contact with Moslem leaders was blocked by the threat of confrontation with Washington and the divisions in Iranian politics that the hostage crisis seemed to deepen. Even though the American hostages were eventually freed, a different group of constraints took their place. From late 1980, the Iran-Iraq war combined with a string of leadership changes in Teheran to prevent a Japanese offer of help on a traditional state-to-state basis.

Tokyo planners thus felt they had no choice but to resort to a nongovernmental instrument—namely, Mitsui. In their judgment, a low-level business linkage via the IJPC would avert high-level conflict while laying the financial foundation for a more reliable Moslem regime. To the Japanese, it was a transnational gamble made risky and inevitable by the environment in which they operated.

Intra-Area Hostility

Antagonism among the Persian Gulf States also underscored the limits of Tokyo's foreign policy. When confronted by warfare between Iran and Iraq or diplomatic split between Saudi Arabia and Libya, the Japanese consistently chose a position of formal neutrality. Such a stance, they felt, would keep Tokyo from being drawn into local hostilities while enabling it to maintain open channels to both contestants.

Unfortunately, a diplomacy of equal distance was inapplicable in the Arab-Israeli conflict. In Japan's view, that struggle did not simply pit one Middle Eastern power against another. Rather, it placed the United States against the Gulf area itself and other members of the Western alliance.

As a superpower and key sponsor of Israel, the United States was thought to be the central force in any long-term solution of the root problem—the Palestinian issue. Although U.S. leaders had espoused support for a comprehensive settlement, they appeared to be headed in a different direction. From Tokyo's perspective, Washington's hands-off policy toward the PLO had yielded a political imbalance, stacking the odds against permanent peace. To help rectify that situation, senior Japanese officials employed a series of approaches aimed at protecting Japan and influencing America.

In the pre–Camp David period, the Japanese initially had used the United Nations and meetings with Middle Eastern leaders to voice their support of Palestinian rights. Moreover, they paved a nondiplomatic path to the PLO through establishment of the Tokyo PLO office.

In the post–Camp David period, however, a more assertive set of policies was required. Because of the partial settlement that resulted, Tokyo officials felt compelled to work with Western Europe, Egypt, and the PLO. Despite differences in geography and politics, the three seemed to have much in common. All of them, the Japanese assumed, had an interest in solving the Palestinian problem and had the potential to reshape Washington's thinking. The EEC was the other major U.S. ally that also depended on foreign oil; Egypt was the Arab country that had staked its future on the success of Camp David; and the PLO seemed to be the outsider that could be brought in if it took the initiative on mutual recognition. What resulted was multilateral movement with the first, stronger bilateral ties to the second, and a nongovernmental invitation to the third in an effort to create a climate conducive to a negotiated peace.

Foreign Intervention

Compounding the first two problems was the threat of superpower intervention. Though pursuing different objectives, both the United States and the Soviet Union were thought to be playing with fire in a strategic tinderbox. Before the U.S. rescue mission in Iran, the Japanese judged that Washington was oblivious to the dangers inherent in a resort to force in the Middle East. In their view, a strike to free the Americans not only could snap the Moslem regime but also could ripen the conditions for Kremlin intervention. Making matters worse was the scenario that was likely to follow.

Whether to take advantage of the hostage crisis or of Iran's continuing slide downward, a Soviet drive from Afghanistan would leave Washington only one desperate option. Given the disrepair of its conventional forces, the United States would have to meet Moscow head-on with a nuclear counterattack. Otherwise, it must be prepared to accept Soviet control over the Strait of Hormuz and the Western economies.

As a result, Tokyo planners formulated policies in early 1980 that would restrain the United States and contain the Soviet Union. On a bilateral basis, they tried to calm Washington through a rejection of Iranian oil and worked to stop Moscow by reducing diplomatic, trade, and cultural relations. Multilaterally, the Japanese joined the EEC in pressuring Teheran to release the American hostages. Finally, through the United Nations and individual contacts, they offered financial aid and diplomatic support to countries in Southwest Asia that were vulnerable to Soviet advance.

In reflecting on these policies, Japanese officials uniformly side-stepped judgments on effectiveness. At the same time, they commonly agreed that what they did fell short of what was required. To close the gap between ideal and reality, the decision makers would need to make a more basic transition.

After 1973, the United States no longer held all the cards for Japanese survival. Nevertheless, it was still Japan's guardian outside the Gulf area and its major impediment in the area. To protect their interests in both areas, senior Japanese officials had to build a new foreign relations matrix that would preserve ties to the Untied States and also integrate the Middle East. For that to happen, they had to reach a comprehensive understanding with Washington on the nature of their relationship.

The United States, the Japanese judged, had consistently refrained from working with them and other members of the Western alliance in confronting problems that it could not solve alone. Although there were calls for common action during the hostage crisis and other emergencies, they were evidently made after the policy lines had already been drawn. Certainly, strong differences on the Middle East existed within the Western alliance. Failure to mediate them, however, would leave the allies at odds among themselves and groping for interim approaches to complex issues.

What seemed to be needed, therefore, was a willingness by Washington to join its friends in defining what their interests were and what their objectives should be, what policies would maximize the chances of diplomatic success, and what role each member could reasonably be expected to play. In Tokyo, such a collective effort would be most welcomed in the hope that it might bring greater world peace—and a stronger partnership with the United States.

Bibliography

Personal Interviews

Amaya, Naohiro, former vice-minister for international affairs, Ministry of International Trade and Industry, July 15, 1980.

Hamid, Fathi Abdul, PLO representative to Tokyo, July 14, 1981.

Hatoytama, Iichiro, former minister of foreign affairs, July 22, 1981.

Hogen, Shinsaku, former vice-minister of foreign affairs, July 16, 1981.

Kimura, Toshio, president of the Japan-Palestine Friendship Commission, July 28, 1981.

Miki, Takeo, former prime minister of Japan, July 29, 1981.

Okita, Saburo, former foreign minister of Japan, July 29, 1981.

Sagami, Takehiro, former vice-minister for international affairs, Ministry of Finance, July 11, 1980.

Shibata, Katsuji, president of the Japan Olympic Committee, July 9, 1980.

Takashima, Masuo, former vice-minister of foreign affairs, July 1, 1980.

Togo, Fumihiko, former Japanese ambassador to the United States, June 25, 1980, and July 21, 1981.

Tsutsumi, Koichi, former deputy director of the Middle East and Southwest Asia Bureau, Ministry of Foreign Affairs, July 2, 1980, and July 17, 1981.

Japanese-Language Materials

Amaya, Watanabe, and Nixon. Articles in *Bungei Shunju,* June 1980. Tokyo: Bungei Shunju, 1980.

Asahi Nenkan. Tokyo: Asahi Shimbunsha, 1974–1982.

Asahi Shimbun (January 1973–December 1982).

Boeicho, *Boei Hakusho, 1982* (Tokyo: Boeicho, 1982).

Hosoya, Chihiro, and Saito, Makoto. *Washington Taisei To Nichibei Kankei.* Tokyo: Tokyo Daigaku Shuppansha, 1978.

Ito, Masaya. *Jiminto Sengokushi.* Tokyo: Asahi Sonorama, 1982.

Kaijo Anpocho. *Kaiho Anpo Hakusho 1982.* Tokyo: Kaijo Anpocho, 1982.

Keizai Kikakucho. *Keizai Hakusho 1982.* Tokyo: Keizai Kikakucho, 1982.

Mainichi Shimbun (June 1978–December 1982).

Nihon Keizai Nenkan. Tokyo: Nihon Keizai Shimbunsha, 1974–1982.

Nihon Keisai Shimbun (March 1979–December 1982).

Okita, Saburo. *Economisuto Gaiso No 252 Nichi.* Tokyo: Toyo Keizai Shimposha, 1980.

———. "Shigen Yunyukoku Nihon O Jikaku Seyo," *Chuo Koron,* December 1967. Tokyo: Chuo Horonsha, 1967.

Togo, Fumihiko. *Nichibei Gaiko Sanjyunen.* Tokyo: Sekai No Ugokisha, 1982.

Tsusho Sangyosho. *Keizai Kyoryoku No Genjo To Mondaiten.* Tokyo: Tsusho Sangyosho, 1982.

Yomiuri Shimbun (January 1982–December 1982).

English-Language Materials

Brzezinski, Zbigniew. "The Failed Mission," *New York Times Magazine,* April 18, 1982.

Christian Science Monitor (September 1981–December 1981).

Curtis, Gerald L. "Japanese Security Policies," *Foreign Affairs,* Spring 1981.

Hurewitz, Jacob C., ed. *Soviet-American Rivalry in the Middle East.* New York: Praeger, 1969.

———. "The Middle East: A Year of Turmoil," *Foreign Affairs,* Winter 1981.

Kissinger, Henry. *The White House Years.* Boston: Little, Brown, 1979. *New York Times.*

Polk, William R. *The Arab World.* Cambridge, Mass.: Harvard University Press, 1980.

Quandt, William D. *Decade of Decisions: American Policy Toward the Arab-Israeli Conflict.* Berkeley: University of California Press, 1977.

W. Quandt, F. Jabber, and A. Lesch. *The Politics of Palestinian Nationalism.* Berkeley: University of California Press, 1973.

Rubinstein, Alvin Z. *Red Star on the Nile: The Soviet-Egyptian Relationship Since the June War* Princeton: Princeton University Press, 1977.

Smith, Middleton, and Weisman. Articles in *America in Captivity: Special Issue of the New York Times Magazine,* May 17, 1981.

Wall Street Journal (September 1981–December 1982).

Washington Post (January 1979–December 1982).

Yoshitsu, Michael M. "Iran and Afghanistan in Japanese Perspective," *Asian Survey,* May 1981.

Index

About the Author

Michael M. Yoshitsu received his B.A. from Stanford University in 1972 and a Ph.D. from Columbia University in 1979. He has been assistant professor of government at the University of Virginia since 1979, and he completed *Caught in the Middle East* while on leave as a visiting Fulbright scholar at the Tokyo University Faculty of Law in 1982. His doctoral dissertation, *Japan and the San Francisco Peace Settlement,* was published by Columbia University Press in 1983, and the Japanese language edition, *Nihon No Dokuritsu* (Japan's Independence), will be released by Kodansha Publishers in 1984. Dr. Yoshitsu's other publications include articles in *The New York Times* and *Asian Survey.*